U.S.-SOVIET DETENTE

U.S.-SOVIET DETENTE: PAST AND FUTURE

Vladimir Petrov

American Enterprise Institute for Public Policy Research
Washington, D. C.

Vladimir Petrov is professor of international affairs at the Institute for Sino-Soviet Studies, The George Washington University,

ISBN 0-8447-3156-0

Foreign Affairs Study 18, April 1975

Library of Congress Catalog Card No. 75-7504

© 1975 by American Enterprise Institute for Public Policy Research, Washington, D. C. Permission to quote from or reproduce material in this publication is granted when due acknowledgment is made.

Printed in the United States of America

CONTENTS

PREFACE

INTRODUCTION — 1
   What Is Detente? 1
   Asymmetry in National Objectives 3

1 U.S.-SOVIET BILATERAL RELATIONS — 7
   Soviet View of the United States 7
   SALT: Soviet Perceptions 9
   Economic Relations 15

2 DETENTE IN THE WORLD AT LARGE — 25
   The Middle East 28
   Oil Embargo 36
   The Cyprus Crisis 40
   Europe 42
   The China Factor 44

3 PROSPECTS FOR DETENTE — 47

APPENDIX — 57

PREFACE

The subject of U.S.-Soviet detente is not susceptible to research in the traditional sense. "Facts" are commonly known to diligent readers of American and Soviet newspapers and to government specialists dealing with specific aspects of U.S.-Soviet relations, such as trade, SALT, the Middle East and Cyprus crises, et cetera. In deciding which "facts" are relevant to the subject, however, and to what extent, analysts and public figures are guided by their own views, political predilections, and the games they are disposed to play. Much less is known about motivations of the protagonists. While a detached analyst can reconstruct President Nixon's considerations with a degree of accuracy, a total secrecy surrounding deliberations and decisions of the Soviet leadership leaves the field open to interpretations frequently resulting in mutually exclusive conclusions.

In these circumstances, I had to rely on my general knowledge of international relations, of Soviet history and Soviet political behavior, on careful reading of specialized Soviet publications, and on numerous and extensive interviews with American officials involved in Soviet affairs and with Soviet scholars and officials involved in American affairs. No one occupied a high enough position to be able to tell me—even if he wanted to—what went on in high councils of his government at any given time; and no one made quotable statements. Yet all of them have in one way or another contributed to my understanding of U.S.-Soviet detente.

The essay which follows contains no "conclusions" or "recommendations." It is an attempt to analyze and appraise detente, particularly as perceived by the Soviets. It is a subjective attempt, in the sense that it reflects my own judgments, and an objective one because I have no particular cause to advocate. There are many disturbing elements in detente: the asymmetries in national perceptions and objectives, the glaring disparities in the processes of foreign policy making, the enormous psychological difficulties the superpowers are having in adjusting to each other in our changing world. The analysis is further handicapped by the difficulty in appraising the impact of international pressures to which Soviet and American policy makers have to respond. Finally, any prognosis is made tenuous by the absence of agreed-upon rules and obligations derived from detente understandings. It often appears as if on the chessboard set before them, one partner would play the game of chess while the other would play checkers; to keep the score of such a game is not an easy task.

Each week brings developments which will affect the progress of Soviet-American detente. Even while this essay has been in preparation, the international climate has continued to evolve. When the manuscript underwent final review in January 1975, however, there had been no developments which would require any substantial alteration of the analysis here presented.

VLADIMIR PETROV
January 1975

INTRODUCTION

What Is Detente?

Detente is a process by which two or more nations move away from a continuous confrontation with each other in the general direction of cooperation. It is a relaxation of international tensions which can take place only when certain objective conditions exist: a realization by the protagonists that there are political and economic limitations to the assertion of their power in the world, a change in the respective national perceptions of the "enemy," and a recognition of the necessity to seek improvement of the nation's posture through a partial accommodation with the adversary.

A common American view notwithstanding, Soviet-American detente does not signify the end of the adversary relationship between the U.S. and the U.S.S.R. Strictly speaking, it only means a rejection of war and a threat of war as the ultimate means of resolving their conflict and achieving their particular objectives; and since the two governments also assume that they can attain these objectives through negotiations, they recognize that their conflict is not irreconcilable or, at the very least, that there are limits to what they can hope to achieve. The initiation of negotiations will not, of course, preclude application of political and economic pressures or exploitation of favorable developments in other countries and regions to the detriment of the adversary. Resort to negotiations, however, does imply that there will be self-restraint and continuous and active diplomatic intercourse.

This definition approximates the understanding the Nixon administration reached with the Soviet leadership as the United States and the Soviet Union embarked on detente some time in 1969. The two governments presented their mutual views in 1972 in a document called "Basic Principles of Relations between the U.S.A. and the U.S.S.R." (see Appendix). Clearly, this document does not provide a set of definable, mutually accepted rules by which the new game is supposed to be played; no document could do that. The document does not enumerate specific obligations detente will impose upon the superpowers, nor does it reflect agreement as to what kind of pressures against the adversary might still be regarded as "fair" or "legitimate."

U.S.-Soviet detente, regardless of definitional problems, will hopefully reduce the danger of nuclear war and promise alleviation of regional conflicts involving the superpowers. It will also create new difficulties, however, by demanding far greater political and diplomatic skill than was required in the "era of confrontation," and by straining the established alliances, as lesser powers anticipate the emergence of a U.S.-Soviet condominium that would sacrifice their vital interests on the altar of detente. New international tensions could arise if these nations begin to attend to their political, economic, and security needs independently. Others, in part because without superpower confrontation the alliances lose much of their initial value to their specific national interests, might become nonaligned or even reverse their original orientation. Such shifts would produce a new instability, subjecting the superpowers, and the detente they initiated, to new pressures. Their resolve to avoid a direct confrontation might not weaken, but their perceptions of each other would continue to change as they attempted to manage, separately or jointly, new local crises.

Furthermore, one finds a disturbing asymmetry in the national perceptions of detente. The Soviets see the global implications of a broad framework for their relations not only with the United States but with Western Europe and Japan as well. They make a distinction between a military and a political detente, relating the former to the issues of strategic arms limitation and reduction in NATO and Warsaw Pact forces, and the latter to cooperation in political, economic and scientific matters. The stated Soviet assumption is that although detente benefits both superpowers (and mankind as a whole), its implementation should not involve substantial sacrifices of national interest or infringement on national sovereignty. But in their perception of the national interest of "imperialists," the Soviets rely on traditional Communist value judgments which lead them to welcome any sign of weakening in the capitalist systems, while simultaneously invoking the concept of national sovereignty as a shield against Western attempts to erode their own internal political base.

There is no defined consensus in the United States—or even within the U.S. government—as to what detente is about, except for the view that it reduces the threat of a nuclear war and promises a reduction of the cost of armaments. The notion of cooperation with the Soviet Union—political or economic—finds few enthusiastic supporters, mainly because of a widespread assumption that the Soviets cannot be trusted, at least until they convincingly prove their goodwill in matters of importance to the U.S.[1] Outside the business community, economic cooperation is viewed by the public as a one-way street, benefiting the Soviets but of minimal advantage to the United States. There is a theory in government and congressional circles that the Soviets have subdued their hostility toward the West only because of their current weakness and a corresponding desire to enhance U.S. advantages at Soviet expense while the going appears good. There is no agreement on the question of ways and means of accomplishing this goal.

Asymmetry in National Objectives

Thus far, the differences in national expectations have not reversed the trend towards detente. Conditions in each country have had the effect of reducing the political influence of those who opposed, for whatever reasons, relaxation of East-West tensions, and of producing a new consensus among the governing elites. The two major factors that contributed to this shift in Moscow have been the stagnation of the Soviet economy and the emerging Chinese threat. The single major factor in the United States was a de facto defeat in Vietnam and the corresponding decline of popular support for an activist foreign policy.[2] These changes have had a marked effect upon the international climate, the intangible but extremely important factor in the conduct of detente diplomacy; yet implementation of specific policies has run into difficulties because of the fundamental asymmetry in the national objectives and assumptions about the contexts in which negotiations could take place. Only one major issue, that of a strategic arms limitation treaty (SALT), could successfully be isolated for bilateral talks between the governments of the United States and

---

[1] Lloyd A. Free, "The International Attitudes of Americans," in Donald R. Lesh, ed., *A Nation Observed* (Washington, D. C.: Potomac Associates, 1974), pp. 133-50. For the official U.S. position, see Secretary Kissinger's statement to the Senate Foreign Relations Committee, *Department of State Bulletin*, no. 1842 (12 October 1974).

[2] Free, "International Attitudes of Americans," p. 144. Also, Walter Laqueur, "From Globalism to Isolationism," *Commentary*, September 1972.

the Soviet Union. The agreement produced by these talks evoked considerable criticism from American opponents of detente, particularly in the Senate. The expansion of bilateral economic relations has been discussed for several years but, because of the congressional opposition, has fallen short of expectations; even the limited trade and lend-lease agreements, signed in Moscow in October 1972, could not be implemented immediately.

While Soviet objectives in detente have required a multilateral approach, the American role in such multilateral activities has been distinctly minor by comparison. In their search for Western participation in developing and modernizing their economy, the Soviets have successfully been negotiating with other governments—mainly Germany, France and Japan. Soviet efforts to reduce tensions in Europe, and, in the process, to undermine NATO, have taken the form of the Conference for Security and Cooperation in Europe (CSCE) in which the United States is only one out of thirty-five participants, none of them subject to a decisive American influence. The parallel negotiations on the reduction of military forces in Europe have been comparatively limited in scope, but even there the Soviet Union can speak more authoritatively for the Warsaw Pact Organization (WPO) than the United States can for NATO.

Specific American objectives in detente have never been fully defined (and perhaps cannot be, given the pluralism of our political system) beyond the disengagement in Southeast Asia and a successful conclusion to the SALT negotiations. The U.S. government has assumed that the Soviets would cooperate in the resolution of the Middle East conflict, although neither the extent of such cooperation nor the Soviet quid pro quo has been subject to formal agreement. Outside the government, there have been expectations and insistence that detente should result in substantial changes in the internal Soviet conditions, such as more tolerance to the dissent of intellectuals, unrestricted emigration of Soviet Jews, and a greater flow of information into the Soviet Union.

Because of this evident divergence in national objectives, the Soviet-American detente can be said to have reached only a preliminary stage. Prolonged negotiations will be required to establish a workable common framework and a greater mutual understanding, and the agreements already reached need to undergo a test of time. One ought not to expect too much from negotiations because the disparity between the methods by which the two political systems form and project national will has been, and is likely to remain, a crucial handicap. In the Soviet Union (and in the People's Republic of China) national will usually means the will of the Communist party leadership. In the United States, any substantial change in national policy requires a large measure of consensus among traditional centers of power: the Congress, the federal bureaucracy involved in foreign affairs, major organized interest groups, the business community, and the press. Even under the best of circumstances, the President would have had difficulty in generating support among these groups for specific detente-related acts of policy. But, as has been amply demonstrated, an administration whose domestic power base had shrunk as a result of a spectacular political scandal faced an impossible task in trying to overcome opposition. The succeeding administration, headed by a President who had not been elected to office but chosen on the grounds of his acceptability to the congressional majority, finds itself in an even worse situation. At the mercy of the fickle moods of legislators and opinion makers, it cannot undertake any significant initiatives in policies toward the Soviet Union and it is unlikely that any new initiatives will occur before the 1976 elections.

The current pause in detente developments may have its advantages. Despite a clear need for greater international cooperation in resolving such critical issues as conflict in the Middle East, worldwide inflation, the questionable cohesiveness of NATO, and the continuing strategic arms build-up, there are powerful arguments for a reassessment of the overall picture. A detached analysis of the Soviet perception of detente and its particular components could help to determine the limits of possible agreements and, in general, to redefine America's role in world affairs. In addition, some judgment needs to be made as to what extent the United States should accommodate— or disregard—the views of its allies and trade partners who consider various aspects of the evolving Soviet-American relationship with apprehension. Finally, there must be a realistic assessment of the nation's readiness to follow the lead of the administration in order to deflate excessive expectations on the one hand, and to dispel unwarranted pessimism on the other.

1

U.S.-SOVIET BILATERAL RELATIONS

Soviet View of the United States

There is probably a universal agreement among the Soviet leaders that, in spite of the current economic reverses, the United States remains the most industrially advanced nation, far richer and more capable of exerting great influence in the world than the Soviet Union. At the same time, they see the United States government itself as relatively weak, subject to a multitude of pressures from diverse economic and political interest groups interlocking with Congress and the federal bureaucracy, known in the Soviet parlance as "ruling circles." Essentially, the Soviets deal only with the presidency; they have no significant means to manipulate these "ruling circles," to influence policies of the United States indirectly.

As seen from Moscow, the United States today is not nearly as powerful as it was a decade ago when it could determine to a large degree policies of other nations, including those of Western Europe and Japan, which were still heavily dependent on it for their security and well-being. Accordingly, the government of the United States today does not have the same voice in world affairs as before. President Nixon was credited with having been "realistic" in recognizing this change, and as having been willing to deal with the Soviet Union on terms of "equality" rather than "from a position of strength" which was the inclination of his predecessors.[1]

Yet the decline of the power of the presidency within the United States, which began in the second Johnson administration, vastly accelerated during the Nixon administration, and is becoming all too

---

[1] For a cogent Soviet analysis, see G. A. Arbatov, "Sovetsko-Amerikanskiye otnosheniya v 70-e gody" [Soviet-American relations in the 1970s], in *S. Sh. A.* [U.S.A.], no. 5 (1974).

obvious in the Ford administration, creates a very special problem for the Soviet Union. While the Soviets have no choice but to negotiate with the President and his representatives, they realize that there are powerful forces at large which influence the administration's foreign policies and severely limit the scope of its understanding with the Soviet Union.[2] In Moscow's view, interaction of these forces accounts for an element of unpredictability in American international behavior, making the establishment of stable Soviet-American relations difficult and calling for a continuous alertness and strong defense posture.

The Soviet leadership regards the United States as a fundamentally hostile nation. In fact, although the American public mood changes from time to time, the underlying anti-Communist, anti-Soviet sentiment remains strong. This is reflected in the general hostility of the press, in the statements and speeches of public figures, in the periodic anti-Soviet demonstrations and abuses of Soviet diplomats, and in the relentless efforts of the military establishment to obtain huge funds for further development and deployment of weapons systems. Although foreign policy judgments clearly are not as black and white today as they were during the years of the cold war, the Soviets see that the United States fairly consistently renders assistance to and sides with nations and political movements hostile to the Soviet Union and Soviet interests.

The Nixon doctrine and President Nixon's detente initiatives were welcome in Moscow, where they were regarded as an indication of the growing realization in the United States of the bankruptcy of policies rooted in cold war concepts and recognition of Soviet ascendancy to strategic parity. But although Moscow greatly preferred the Nixon-Kissinger team to that of Johnson and Rusk, it would be a grave mistake to conclude that the Soviet leaders became completely trusting of the Nixon administration.[3] The opening of communications with Peking at a time of extreme tension in Soviet-Chinese relations, the bombing of North Vietnam and the mining of

---

[2] This development has been almost universally recognized and has been articulately expressed by many analysts; for example: "The whole series of events, including Vietnam and Watergate and economic slippage has eroded the power of the president in foreign affairs. He does not receive traditional deference." Steven S. Rosenfeld, "Pluralism and Policy," *Foreign Affairs*, January 1974.

[3] The Soviets would wholeheartedly agree with Robert W. Tucker ("The American Outlook: Change and Continuity," in Robert E. Osgood, ed., *Retreat from Empire* [Baltimore: Johns Hopkins University Press, 1973], pp. 50-51) that the Nixon administration had not abandoned the containment of communism as a primary goal of American policy.

the Haiphong harbor on the eve of Nixon's first visit to Moscow, the continuing military assistance to Israel necessitating the costly shipments of Soviet supplies to Egypt and Syria, the strategic forces alerts during the Jordanian crisis in September 1970, and the Middle East war in October 1973—all these and many less spectacular acts of the United States government have indicated that a genuine "peaceful coexistence" is far off, and that the fundamental American anti-Sovietism remains a crucial factor of international life.

Yet balancing this tendency, the Nixon and Ford administrations have displayed enough credible interest in the lowering of tensions in bilateral Soviet-American relations to give grounds for a degree of optimism among the Soviet ruling elite. There were, and still are, elements that can be called neo-Stalinist in the top of the Soviet hierarchy, who have argued against significant concessions to the emerging spirit of detente, insisting on an ideologically hostile posture vis-à-vis "imperialists," and on employing every possible means for weakening the United States and its alliances. On the other side of the spectrum, however, have been those who pressed for greater cooperation with the West for the sake of reducing military expenditures and obtaining the sorely needed means for modernization of the Soviet economy, and those who believed that a lowered pitch in anti-American propaganda would produce more relaxed attitudes in the United States and thereby contribute to a greater security for the Soviet Union.

It would be erroneous to assume that the issue of Soviet-American relations primarily determines the configuration of political forces in the Soviet Union; domestic determinants, including opposition to excessive relaxation of vigilance, are more important. From the beginning, however, the less ideologically oriented elements clearly predominated in the Politburo's discussions. It was only toward the end of 1973 that the combined effects of the Jackson amendment syndrome, the Watergate scandal, and the October War caused a shift of the ruling consensus toward a harder position.

SALT: Soviet Perceptions

The key to understanding the Soviet position on SALT is Moscow's relentless preoccupation with the physical security of the Soviet Union. It would be pointless to argue that no one threatens that country, that the United States would never launch a nuclear attack, that the Chinese are much weaker than the Russians and would remain so for decades to come, or that NATO forces pose no danger to the Warsaw Pact. Soviet attitudes of mistrust toward "imperialists," born in the early years of the Soviet Republic and reinforced by the international isolation of the interwar period, were greatly heightened by the traumatic impact of the German invasion. Thus it was nearly irrelevant that in the end Russia emerged victorious, defeating its two principal enemies, Germany and Japan. What mattered was that the Germans almost succeeded in crushing the Soviet resistance, and that victory was achieved at a tremendous human and material sacrifice.

While the Soviet armies were still moving into the heart of Europe, combatting Nazi forces, recognition of a new external enemy was already evolving in Moscow. The United States, emerging out of the war intact, with greatly increased economic power and new imperial ambition, was a natural leader of all forces opposing communism and fearing Soviet power. For the last quarter of a century, the Soviets have never stressed, not even for propaganda purposes, that in the Second World War the United States was a friend and ally of Russia. It is a matter of faith in Moscow that by delaying the opening of the second front in Europe the United States (and Great Britain) sought a maximum weakening of Russia in its momentous struggle against Germany. Soviet leaders believe that the bombings of Dresden, Hiroshima and Nagasaki were meant to demonstrate the superiority of the new strategic power of the United States, and that the essential aim of the "containment" policy of the cold war era was to isolate the Soviet Union and deny it a major role in world affairs. They feel that the changes in international environment of recent years have not been a result of change of heart on the part of "imperialists" but are the product of the Vietnam calamity, the transformation of relations within NATO, the deepening economic crisis in the West, and the reality of the growing strategic power of the Soviet Union. Whatever the effect of these influences, the question remained: to what extent could the change in international environment be regarded as irreversible?

There is a strong consensus among the Soviet leaders that given a drastic turn of events such as a disintegration of the Warsaw Pact Organization, a flare-up in Sino-Soviet hostility, or some serious internal crisis leading to the weakening of the Soviet state, the "imperialists" would not miss a chance to make matters worse by advancing the cause of "freedom" and "democracy" in Russia. Even if they perceived President Nixon as likely to exercise self-restraint in such a situation, the Soviet leaders are not at all sure that subsequent presidents will not take a very different attitude.

The assumption of the continuing rivalry between the two global powers representing two conflicting political systems makes it impossible for the Soviets to even begin considering the United States as trustworthy enough to make the security of the Soviet Union subject to treaties and agreements with it.[4] Soviet secretiveness and cunning in SALT negotiations are well known. Some may regard these traits as manifestation of a traditional Russian paranoia. The fact is that for compelling historical reasons, the Soviets act this way quite naturally, trusting neither friend nor foe, and seeing an additional source of strength in preserving their secrets.

Moreover, as they discuss strategic arms limitations with the United States, the Soviets constantly keep in mind that one day they may also be confronted by the hostile and dangerous power of China, a subject excluded from SALT negotiations but of obvious relevance to the Soviet position. Enough has been said in the United States, and said on a high enough level (although never officially by the White House), about playing the "Chinese card" against the Soviet Union—viewing China as a potential partner in some future conflict [5]—to make the Soviets reckon very seriously with such a possibility; and the Soviets have no doubts that this very possibility was in the minds of the Chinese leaders as they abandoned their virulent anti-Americanism and embarked on an unambiguous anti-Soviet course in their internal and external policies during the early 1970s. It has always been a working assumption in Moscow that enemies of the Soviet Union have a natural tendency to gravitate toward each other.

A desire to slow down the armaments race, and thereby reduce the back-breaking costs of this economically unproductive expenditure, is doubtless present among segments of the Soviet elite. If there were less of a capacity in the West to take advantage of Soviet weaknesses, this desire would be stronger and more likely to result in a relaxed defense posture. For the time being, however, national security retains priority, leaving little room for substantial concessions.

There are other obstacles to a comprehensive bilateral SALT agreement. The principle of "parity" and even the more elusive principle of "substantial equality" have been recognized formally in

---

[4] See the article by the deputy chief of the international department of the CC CPSU, V. V. Zagladin, "Na novom istoricheskom etape" [Along the new historical path], in *Voprosy istorii KPSS* [Problems of CPSU history], no. 6 (1974).

[5] See, for instance, Henry M. Jackson, *China and American Policy*, Report to the Committee on Armed Forces, U.S. Senate (Washington, D. C.: Government Printing Office, 1974).

Washington and, provided allowances are made for Soviet defense needs in the Far East, further mutual adjustments in nuclear capacities and means of delivery could be gained. But what of qualitative "parity"? Given the continuing secret search for new technological breakthroughs and a refusal—on both sides—to contemplate on-site inspection, an agreement in this area is most unlikely. This will be true until each side concludes that further efforts to refine existing weapons systems, or to develop new ones, are simultaneously dangerous and costly, and generally counterproductive.

Finally, there is a question of the individual strategies which the two superpowers envision for fighting an ultimate war. The inherent purpose of military strategy is to outmaneuver the enemy by the most effective employment of the available forces and means of defense. A mere knowledge of physical capabilities of the enemy is insufficient to meet every conceivable contingency. Each side has to outguess the other while keeping a few surprises up its sleeve. As a result, the secrecy shrouding strategic planning acquires paramount importance and military establishments employ various means to mislead any would-be enemy as to the actual strategy they are pursuing. As Secretary of Defense Schlesinger complained recently:

> The Soviets have not proved . . . communicative about their programs and motives, and the evidence of what they are up to is . . . fragmentary and conflicting. As so often is the case, we are faced with uncertainty. My counterparts in the Soviet Ministry of Defense could substantially reduce this uncertainty by disclosing current and even past information about their decisions to the same extent that the United States does.[6]

This statement does not take into account Soviet thinking on the subject. For one thing, partial disclosures—even if they are honest—can be very misleading, and the Soviets, perhaps not without reason, take with a grain of salt whatever disclosures are made by the Pentagon. For another, considering themselves militarily weaker than the United States and its allies, the Soviets have no urge whatsoever to put their cards on the table and reveal, even if in a very rough outline, their military-political strategy. Thus, although the particular game of arms limitation is not played by the same rules, reticence exists on both sides, handicapping SALT negotiations; each side can only guess what the actual motives and plans of the adversary may be.

---

[6] U.S. Department of Defense, *Annual Defense Department Report, FY 1975*, p. 29.

It is generally accepted, for example, that the United States's nuclear strategy is based on the principle of deterrence—on maintaining second-strike capability sufficient to devastate an enemy who might launch a nuclear attack, thereby discouraging it from attempting such folly. There is no parallel effort to assure survival of the nation if an attack takes place. The U.S. government has virtually abandoned the projects designed to provide for civil defense, and for defense against enemy ICBMs, and is phasing down what has existed in the area of air defense.

The Soviets, on the other hand, while building up their capacity for attack, also place considerable emphasis (and expend sizeable resources which could be used for economic development) on assuring a partial survival in case of an enemy nuclear attack. The question that unsettles American strategic planners is whether or not the Soviets are actually preparing for the unthinkable. It is true that in the 1972 ABM treaty the Soviets gave up the possibility of an ABM defense of their country, but whether they did so because their ABMs were inferior to the task (we knew that they were inferior, and the Soviets knew that we knew it) or because they had embraced the American concept of assured mutual destruction, no one can tell with certainty. The Soviets themselves do not say what their *true* views on the subject are, but they continue research and development of defense capability, providing rationale for the United States to do the same.[7]

In its turn, the U.S. keeps the Soviets guessing. On 27 March 1974, during Secretary Kissinger's visit to Moscow, Secretary of Defense Schlesinger made a statement to the effect that the United States intended to increase its strategic options by retargeting some of its ICBMs. Moscow could have interpreted this as a departure from the concept of assured mutual destruction and as an attempt to make nuclear war thinkable.[8] The Soviets take for granted that we are not

---

[7] Russian expenditure on defense against nuclear attack may have a very simple explanation. To a Russian mind, preparation for war makes no sense unless there is a possibility that war might take place. If there is such a possibility, the Politburo would feel that its special obligations to the several million people who constitute that country's ruling elite would require provision for at least a modicum of capacity for survival. In our view, they may be wasting scarce resources trying to achieve the impossible. But this is only our view.

[8] U.S. Department of Defense, *Annual Defense Department Report, FY 1975*, p. 4. Arguing that "we do not intend that the Soviet Union should have a wider range of options than we do," Secretary Schlesinger stressed that "the Soviet Union now has the capability . . . to undertake selective attacks other than cities." It is easy to imagine that, reporting to the Politburo of the CC CPSU, the Soviet secretary of defense would also assert that it is the United States that

really bound by any stated concept, and they must wonder what was *truly* on Schlesinger's mind when he was delivering his speech.

The conclusion appears inescapable that so long as Soviet and American strategic thinking is not brought into some sort of balance and the element of surprise is not abandoned as an integral part of preparation for war, no reasonable foundation for a comprehensive agreement is likely to be built.

There is another dimension to SALT, not much spoken about, that is also crucial to the understanding of the Soviet reluctance to move towards a comprehensive agreement. "Parity" may sound well, but given each nation's 20:1 factor in its capacity to destroy the other, does it assure an equal self-restraint of the superpowers in conflict situations? A nuclear war may never take place, but use of a nuclear threat for coercion remains a possibility. Khrushchev tried it when he ordered the missiles to be placed in Cuba, as did Kennedy when he forced Khrushchev to take them away. In September 1970, President Nixon ordered a strategic alert and flew to the Sixth Fleet in the Mediterranean to impress upon the Soviets the need to force Syria to call off an attack on Jordan. In October 1973, a new alert was ordered, this time worldwide, to discourage the Soviets from sending their forces to Egypt, whose defense against the Israelis was collapsing.

As the Soviets see it, such recent moves may have been bluffs, but very dangerous bluffs, not to be called easily, given the generally erratic (in their view) behavior of the United States government. These incidents were convincing proofs that, detente rhetoric notwithstanding, the United States had not quite given up its disposition to deal with the Soviet Union "from a position of strength." And if such is the case, how strong an argument in Moscow can be made by those who favor strategic arms limitation? Of course, the Soviets have themselves been past masters of coercive diplomacy (vis-à-vis China, for instance, after 1969, not to mention Hungary in 1956 or Czechoslovakia in 1968), but few national leaders think that what's sauce for the goose is sauce for the gander. Besides, the present Soviet leaders believe that their own employment of military forces for political ends had nothing to do with detente with the United States; it was limited to countries outside U.S. security zones.

All this is not to say that SALT negotiations must be inherently fruitless and should be abandoned. As the two delegations meet in

---

has "a wider range of options" and insist on developing additional capabilities for Soviet forces. In the absence of a detached referee, such arguments can go on indefinitely.

endless sessions to discuss the unthinkable, a kind of common framework gradually evolves, providing for a better comprehension of the other side's thinking, and indirectly contributing to the general feeling of security. But insofar as the Soviets are concerned, a substantive accord would require objective conditions much more disadvantageous to the United States than those extant. In the meantime, they are likely to bide their time, conceding a bit here and there in minor agreements—to keep the spirit of detente alive—but consenting to nothing which might conceivably result in an increased relative advantage to the United States, to NATO, or to the People's Republic of China. The agreement signed by President Ford and General Secretary Brezhnev after their meeting in Vladivostok in November 1974 fully supports this conclusion.[9]

Economic Relations

Broadening of economic relations between the United States and the Soviet Union has from the outset been regarded as an integral part of detente. Soviet-American trade had been stagnant for years; the turnover in 1970 amounted to about $200 million, less than one-half of 1 percent of the total U.S. trade and about 3 percent of the total Soviet trade with the West. A desire to expand trade relations was based on valid considerations on both sides. Because of the compelling need to modernize their economy, the Soviets had abandoned the old concept of autarky and since the late 1960s were expanding their economic ties with advanced industrial nations at an impressive rate. For its part, the Nixon administration attached great importance to international trade. From a level of $67.3 billion in 1968, the total foreign trade turnover went to almost $180 billion in 1973. Government economists and segments of the business community regarded the Soviet Union, as well as the People's Republic of China and the socialist countries of Eastern Europe, as potentially promising markets. But in order to expand trade with the Soviet Union, serious obstacles had to be overcome. One of these was the question of credits: the Soviets had little they could sell in order to pay for imports, and their capacity for exporting to the United States was further limited by discriminatory tariffs which denied to them (and to other socialist countries, save for Yugoslavia and Poland) the traditional most-favored-nation (MFN) status. Another obstacle was political: in the "era of confrontation," few American businessmen

---

[9] See Secretary Kissinger's press conference of 7 December 1974.

would consider taking risks of trading with the enemy. Finally, to the leaders of both countries, the idea of economic interdependence appeared difficult to swallow.

As the concept of detente began to take shape, the two governments reconsidered old attitudes. The negotiations following President Nixon's visit to Moscow in May 1972 resulted in an economic package that took the form of two interrelated executive agreements, signed on 18 October 1972. These provided for the settlement of the lend-lease debt (repayment by the Soviets of $722 million, over thirty years), a Soviet pledge to triple trade volume over the next three years, operating privileges for U.S. corporations and, in exchange, most-favored-nation treatment. The removal of the legislative ban on MFN by the Congress was a precondition for bringing the agreements into full effect. An important part of the economic package was President Nixon's commitment to make available to the Soviet Union long-term (over five years), relatively low-interest Export-Import Bank credits, normally required to make U.S. exports competitive with those of other industrial nations.

Indirect government subsidies to exporters have long been standard practice in the modern world. In addition to export insurance and guarantees to the exporters against nonpayments, all major countries have been offering purchasers credits for up to fifteen years at rates ranging from $5\frac{1}{2}$ percent to $8\frac{1}{4}$ percent; the current United States "mix" of a typical commercial and Eximbank credit rates (by statute, Eximbank can put up no more than 45 percent of the total) is currently about 10 percent. Such subsidized credit rates usually apply to the exports of machinery and other capital goods; sales of commodities and consumer goods are financed by short-term credits at much higher commercial rates.

To a detached observer of international trade, the economic package negotiated in Moscow appeared unspectacular. The projected growth was modest. Aside from the Soviet commitment to settle the wartime debt (which they had been reluctant to do on the grounds that similar debts of other American allies had been written off a long time ago), there were no serious concessions made on either side. It seemed that since there existed a mutual desire to expand economic relations, the United States decided to terminate discriminatory practices and to regard the Soviet Union as it would any other trade partner. The Soviets, having no reason to discriminate against American trade to begin with, merely concurred.

Yet long before the Moscow agreements had borne fruit, the economic package became a subject of controversy in the United States.

Business analysts and partisans of anti-Soviet causes were quick to point out that the Soviets would gain much more than the United States. They would be purchasing machinery and sophisticated equipment, not consumer goods. As they imported whole plants, they would obtain the valuable modern technology; they would develop their natural resources, expand their petrochemical industry, and increase—even if only at some future date—their competitiveness in world markets. And most of this would be done on credit partially subsidized by the American taxpayer. Benefits to the United States, on the other hand, were perceived as marginal. The settlement of the nettlesome lend-lease debt, although welcome, was not regarded as crucial, and the promise of improvement in the employment picture received little attention. A favorable trade balance, although strengthening the nation's balance of payments, was dismissed as nearly irrelevant because most of the sales would be on credit. The rationale for creating additional jobs in the plants of the corporations trading with Russia seemed to be offset by the AFL-CIO argument that exporting capital goods to any country means loss of jobs to the American workingmen. And although the Soviets have had a perfect record of paying their bills, it has been stressed time and again that they do not have, and are unlikely to have in the foreseeable future, enough exportable goods to pay for their imports. Critics argue that the promise of joint ventures in the development of Russia's natural resources is too uncertain to warrant heavy U.S. involvement.

It has been quite clear from the beginning of the debate that the issues involved were not discussed on their merits, and that political, rather than economic, considerations dominated the arguments of those who opposed the deal.[10] The major concern was that the United States would, in effect, assist in building the economic power of its principal enemy and, additionally, that some of the equipment the

---

[10] Some examples: The hearings before the House Ways and Means Committee where witnesses opposing trade with the Soviets included representatives of such political groups as the National Captive Nations Committee. *Congressional Digest*, November 1973, pp. 268-270; testimonies of Walter Laqueur and Leopold Labedz, in *Negotiation and Statecraft*, GPO nos. 94-229 and 98-203, on 17 April 1973 and 17 July 1974, respectively; Hearings before the Joint Economic Committee, 17-19 July 1973; *Soviet Economic Outlook*, GPO 23-245; Harvey D. Shapiro, "Alexei Kosygin Has a Friend at Chase Manhattan," *New York Times Magazine*, 24 February 1974; Marshall I. Goldman, "Who Profits More from U.S.-Soviet Trade?" *Harvard Business Review*, November 1973, pp. 79-87. Specific arguments against granting the Soviet Union MFN status are enumerated and deflated by Raymond Vernon, "Apparatchiks and Enterpreneurs: U.S.-Soviet Economic Relations," *Foreign Affairs*, January 1974. For a comprehensive evaluation of Soviet economic considerations in detente, see Alec Nove, "Can We Buy Detente?" *New York Times Magazine*, 13 October 1974.

Soviets would purchase could increase their military might as well. Relatively few politicians spoke up against detente itself; the administration's general policy enjoyed broad popular endorsement. Instead, the opposition exploited the common misperception that detente would end the rivalry between the superpowers and that the Soviets would begin to accommodate American interests. It was easy for the ever-critical press to demonstrate that rather than becoming more cooperative, the Soviets continued to act against these interests on a global scale. Russia was accused of trying to drive a wedge between the United States and its allies and to squeeze American influence out of Europe. The press emphasized that in the Middle East the U.S.S.R. sided with the enemies of Israel, and that, the SALT agreements notwithstanding, they proceeded building up their military power. The massive Soviet grain purchases in the summer and fall of 1972, which resulted in a sizeable increase in American wheat and feed-grain prices, facilitated the task of the opposition. Conducted in the accepted business tradition of secrecy to assure more favorable prices, the Soviet transactions were widely interpreted as inimical to the American consumer. The administration was roundly accused of putting detente ahead of its duty to the American people and of doing special favors for grain exporters.[11]

The principal effort to block development of U.S.-Soviet economic relations took place in Congress, where the debate over the Trade Reform Act, introduced by the administration in 1973, became an instrument for scuttling detente. Several amendments, sponsored by heavy majorities of legislators in both houses, purported to redress the imbalance of the economic package negotiated in Moscow by attaching to the Trade Reform Act certain political conditions. The Jackson-Vanik amendment, for example, demanded unrestricted emigration for Soviet Jews as a condition for extension of MFN treatment to the Soviet Union. Others sought to block Eximbank credits to Communist countries that deny freedom of religion, conscience, and emigration to their citizens, and obstruct international arms limitation and troop reduction negotiations.

---

[11] Goldman, "Who Profits More?" *New York Times*, 19 September 1972, reported that subsequent to Soviet purchases the price of wheat jumped from $1.32 per bushel to $1.70. In 1974, however, without Soviet purchases, wheat prices fluctuated around $5. At the time of the purchase, the transaction was attacked by a great number of politicians, including Senators McGovern, Jackson, Byrd, Bentsen, Symington, and Representatives Purcell, Rosenthal, and Melcher. See also U.S. Congress, Senate, Permanent Subcommittee on Investigations of the Committee on Government Operations, *Hearings on Russian Grain Transactions*, 20, 23, and 24 July, 9 October 1973, and 8 October 1974. Testimony of Secretary of Agriculture Earl L. Butz was heard on 23 July 1973.

Because of initial high hopes, Soviet reaction to the campaign against expansion of economic relations predictably has been bitter.[12] Moscow does not consider valid the question of Soviet ability to export in order to pay for imports from the United States. The Soviets point out that their foreign obligations are backed by the whole economic might of Russia and that they have not yet defaulted on any contracts or payments. Statements of Soviet officials indicate that Russia regards the question of where it would find the funds to pay its debts as nobody's business.

The Soviets also argue that U.S.-Soviet trade, even if expanded as envisioned, would only be a fraction of their total trade with the capitalist world which, in 1972, reached a total of 9 billion rubles. The statistics tend to confirm their argument (see Table 1).

Because of the grain purchases, the U.S.-Soviet trade turnover increased sharply in 1973. The Soviets bought $1,190 million worth of goods while selling $214 million, thus providing close to $1 billion of trade surplus—more than any other trading partner of the United States. The first half of 1974, however, showed a marked decline in comparison with 1973 because of lower Soviet purchases and greater U.S. imports from Russia.

The principal Soviet response to the arguments of the American opponents of broader trade relations is that, aside from grain, there is relatively little of what they can buy in this country that they cannot obtain elsewhere—in Germany, Japan, France, or Great Britain. These countries do not seem to share the fear that they may be contributing to the Soviet economic growth, and are actively seeking Soviet trade. Moscow further argues that detente or no detente, trade would not expand unless both partners see it as mutually beneficial; it rejects the notion that by trading with Russia, the United States is doing it special favors. Finally, some Soviet officials take the line that their country has managed to survive and expand its economy for fifty years without foreign cooperation, and, if political conditions are not conducive to economic detente, Russia would be able to continue on its own.

Soviet insistence on MFN has been based on political considerations: the U.S. ban on MFN has become a symbol of discrimination, incompatible with detente policy. As to the question of financing, because of the skyrocketing commercial rates, the absence of Eximbank credits would effectively preclude most Soviet purchases. In spite of greater earnings from oil exports, potential surpluses from trading

---

[12] Interview with Soviet Minister of Foreign Trade N. S. Patolichev, in *S.Sh.A.* [U.S.A.], no. 5 (1974).

Table 1
TRADE TURNOVER AND SOVIET EXPORTS
(rubles in millions)

Countries	Year	Total	Exports
United Kingdom	1971	605	405
	1972	558	371
	1973	715	541
Italy	1971	495	233
	1972	464	228
	1973	614	310
France	1971	774	377
	1972	816	381
	1973	722	272
Japan	1971	734	377
	1972	816	382
	1973	994	622
Canada	1971	149	12
	1972	300	19
	1973	265	21
United States	1971	184	54
	1972	538	76
	1973	1161	138
West Germany	1971	667	255
	1972	827	256
	1973	1210	454
East Germany	1971	3443	1716
(excluding West Berlin)	1972	3706	1671
	1973	3965	1856

Source: Data according to the Bureau of East-West Trade, Department of Commerce.

with other hard currency nations simply would not be big enough to pay for American imports in cash. But disappointed as they might have been, the Soviets indignantly rejected suggestions that they ought to make political concessions as a price for the privilege of trading with the United States. Although, given the right atmosphere, they could make—as they have in the past—an occasional gesture of goodwill to improve their image in this country, any kind of formal linkage between the issues they consider unrelated has always been a stumbling block in negotiating with the Soviets. This has particularly been true when they felt that the issue involved their sovereign right to conduct their internal affairs as they saw fit.

Aside from purely economic considerations, the Soviets wanted to expand trade with the United States for three additional reasons. One was that a large-scale American involvement in the development of the Soviet economy would remove the last inhibitions of some of the American allies (for example, Japan) which had thus far been reluctant to conclude major deals with Russia on their own. Another was the hope that, as more business contacts were created, the ability of the business community in this country to counteract trends inimical to Soviet interests would increase. Finally, along with President Nixon, the Soviet leaders believed that stronger economic ties, although not in themselves guaranteeing eternal peace, would serve as a major underpinning of detente between the two countries.

These reasons notwithstanding, the prospect at the moment is that, instead of expanding, U.S.-Soviet trade will contract, perhaps drastically. Current economic dislocations in advanced industrial nations due to inflation, the energy crisis, and declining growth rates make long-term trade relations less predictable. Although benefiting from higher oil prices, the Soviet Union would doubtless suffer from the growing worldwide shortage of credit, caused in part by the flow of huge amounts of funds to the oil-producing countries. Caught in a crunch, Western corporations would be more likely to stick to familiar markets than try to develop a new one in the Soviet Union. This pessimistic outlook is tacitly recognized in Moscow, while the renewed talk in the U.S.S.R. about the "aggravation of the general crisis of capitalism" reflects current Soviet perceptions of the overall situation.[13]

Other causes for a probable contraction of U.S.-Soviet trade are political. The recent bill extending the Eximbank's lending authority provided for a $300 million ceiling on the credits to the Soviet Union for the next four years, a clearly discriminatory measure designed to discourage large-scale trade and the more ambitious development projects in Russia. To a much greater extent, however, the Soviet decision in January 1975 not to bring the 1972 U.S.-U.S.S.R. trade agreement into force was determined by the inclusion of the Jackson amendment in the final version of the Trade Reform Act. Fully aware of the need for give-and-take, the Soviets had repeatedly let it be

---

[13] N. Inozemtsev, "Kapitalism 70-kh godov: obostreniye protivorechii" [Capitalism in the 1970s: aggravation of contradictions], *Pravda*, 20 August 1974.

known—privately—that they were willing to follow a more liberal policy regarding the Jewish emigration issue, but, in the trade negotiations, had never linked it with economic issues.

The 18 October 1974 publication of the Kissinger-Jackson exchange of "assurances" and "understandings," making the MFN status and Eximbank credits to the Soviet Union contingent upon the expansion of Jewish emigration, with a then-potential presidential candidate, Senator Jackson, claiming a major political victory over the Soviets, created, in Moscow's view, an intolerable situation involving national prestige. To acquiesce in this matter would be tantamount to admitting defeat by the forces in America openly and implacably hostile to the Soviet Union, to allowing the United States, in effect, to legislate policies of the Soviet government.

On 26 October 1974, Soviet Foreign Minister Gromyko, in a letter to Kissinger, denounced in unmistakable terms the linkage of the two issues.[14] Badly wanting the passage of the Trade Reform Act for a number of reasons of overriding importance and unable to bend the will of the congressional opposition, the administration disregarded the implicit warning contained in Gromyko's letter. Shortly before the Christmas recess, the trade act, incorporating the Jackson amendment, was passed by the Congress.

The Soviet policy-making machinery went into action. The Politburo reported the situation to the December Plenum of the Central Committee of the CPSU and apparently won endorsement for a tough stand on the issue. On 10 January 1975, one week after the President signed the trade act into law, the Soviet government informed the United States that it regarded this legislation as contravening the 1972 trade agreement and the principle of noninterference in domestic affairs, and that for these reasons it had decided not to put the agreement into force. Simultaneously, it repudiated all the "assurances" on the Jewish emigration question, declaring the latter as being entirely within the Soviet domestic jurisdiction. Among other casualties of the episode was the Soviet obligation to pay the balance of the agreed-upon lend-lease debt, some $660 million, such payments being linked to the extension to the Soviet Union of the MFN treatment.[15]

As a result of these developments the Soviets would have to reappraise their plans, scale down their expectations, and revise their import priorities. Large-scale projects would probably have to be postponed indefinitely and most of their trade redirected to those

---

[14] TASS statement, 19 December 1974.

[15] The secretary of state's press conference, 14 January 1975.

countries—such as France, Germany, Japan, and Great Britain—which do not mix trade with politics. The United States would be left with an even smaller share of Communist trade but with the satisfaction of not contributing to economic growth and general well-being of its principal adversary.

countries—such as France, Germany, Japan, and Great Britain—which do not mix trade with politics. The United States would be left with an even smaller share of Communist trade but with the satisfaction of not contributing to economic growth and general well-being of its principal adversary.

2

DETENTE IN THE WORLD AT LARGE

It goes without saying that the U.S.-Soviet detente is only one factor in international affairs of the modern world, and not necessarily the decisive one. The tremendous upsurge of nationalism, the diminishing dependence of so many states on superpower protection and economic aid (and the diminishing will and capacity of the superpowers to help) have limited the impact of detente upon the lives of other nations. The "two camps" are still there, competing with and opposing each other, functioning autonomously, maintaining their particular value systems and preserving the economic, political, and security links between members. But these links are not what they used to be. There are growing strains within each camp, and centrifugal forces are at work, increasingly challenging unity of purpose and the primacy of the superpower. More often, members of the opposing camps communicate, trade, and treat with each other, following the call of opening opportunities rather than dictates of ideologies. And there is, of course, a large body of states which belong to neither camp and do not follow the leadership of any great power.

The Soviet-American detente has contributed to the complexities of the political-military relationships by relieving fears among Western and nonaligned nations of the "Communist menace." It has suggested to many governments that if the United States and the Soviet Union could be on speaking terms, so could they. Even before SALT, the credibility of American nuclear protection had fallen under question, notably by the French, and our allies have noted the domestic pressures, originated during the Vietnam war, for reducing U.S. overseas commitments. They have thus been encouraged to hedge their bets by normalizing and expanding their relations with the Soviet Union and the People's Republic of China, the latter still relatively inactive in world affairs but viewed as a potential counterbalance to the former by those who regard Russia a major strategic threat. Similarly, governments of some member-nations of the Soviet bloc, having come to fear less subversion and potential threat of the West, have developed lively interest in forming connections with capitalist countries. While the more insecure and exposed regimes (North Korea, North Vietnam, East Germany, and Cuba) still strongly espouse the concept of Communist unity, and while others, having been reminded of Soviet power by the invasion of Czechoslovakia, continue to heed much of Moscow's advice in their external affairs, the cohesion of the Soviet camp is clearly not what it once was. Ruling Communist elites now view Western trade and tourism as beneficial and even welcome. There is even a resurgence of pride in historical links with Western culture.

For fear of giving them additional impetus, the Communists avoid acknowledging these trends. Nevertheless, both the Soviet Union and the United States recognize them and they directly affect detente developments. On both sides there is concern with preserving influence in one's domain and apprehension lest the security alliances break down before detente bears fruit. In the present transitional phase, domestic political misgivings and awareness that the world has become much less manageable produce a countertrend to the sentiment for avoiding confrontations and reducing the danger of a nuclear war. Aggravating the situation is another critical asymmetry of Soviet and American detente strategies.

For the United States, detente primarily concerns the state of relations with the Soviet Union and the People's Republic of China. Relations with the other Communist states are essentially seen as derivatives of detente. The states themselves appear relatively unimportant except in so far as they are part of the Communist world which we want to see divided and weakened.

The Soviet view of detente is quite different and far more complex. To Moscow, there is not only one detente with the United States, but many: with France and Germany, Canada and Turkey, Iran and Japan, as well as with lesser capitalist nations. A key principle of Soviet diplomacy is to deal with them as separate and sovereign entities rather than as allies of the United States. Although they realize the influence of the United States upon its allies' foreign policies, the Soviets also believe that in the long run external behavior of a nation is determined by internal factors. Thus their strategy is dual: to accentuate the positive in bilateral relations and benefit from them economically and politically, while taking full advantage of what they see as the existing and developing "contradictions in the imperialist camp." Thus, while the United States habitually focuses its apprehension on Soviet power, perceiving no serious danger from other members of the Soviet bloc, the Soviets see their security enhanced by visible weakening of our alliances and are alert to every opportunity of contributing to this process.

There is another significant difference between the two nations which affects detente relationships. As the Soviets open up communications with the outside world, their impulse to protect the home base from subversive Western influences becomes stronger. They are concerned with internal security of Russia and they constantly encourage vigilance in other Communist countries. Since all Communist leaders basically share this impulse and regard internal security of paramount importance, they keep contacts with the West under tight control. Similarity of such political instincts accounts for much of what is left of Soviet bloc unity vis-à-vis the West.

Needless to say, in this respect the United States differs fundamentally from the Soviet Union. Its alliances are much more like partnerships. Originally founded on the fear of communism and Soviet power, their cohesion diminished in proportion to the diminution of this fear. Ideals of democracy and free enterprise—perceived differently everywhere—do not provide a sufficient bond, and nationalism remains an accepted fact of life. The ability of the United States to impose cohesiveness upon the non-Communist world is negligible, and it can do nothing to protect allied nations from the internal crises resulting from political demoralization or Communist influences.

Communist ideology provides Soviet international behavior with a uniquely peculiar framework in yet another way. With or without detente, the Soviet Union would always be predicted to side, at least politically, with "anticolonialist" Third World nations, and voice support for widely varied anti-Western causes and "national-liberation" movements. This essentially ideological commitment has survived numerous disappointments and setbacks and cannot be abandoned, no matter how important it might be for Moscow to court the goodwill of the United States and other Western nations. The Soviets can—and do—regulate the pitch of their propaganda and allow themselves considerable leeway as to what they actually *do* in supporting "progressive" movements and harming Western interests. To this extent, recent Soviet actions have been determined by detente —which, incidentally, is the principal accusation the Maoists level against Soviet "revisionism." But although this pragmatic attitude, reinforced by imperatives of superpower interests, may become more pronounced with the passage of time, to expect the Soviets to stop preaching what they have been preaching since 1917 is tantamount to expecting them to stop being Communists.

Soviet commitment to anti-Western causes has been regarded in the United States as not only inimical to American interests but fundamentally incompatible with detente. In the Soviet view, this latter assessment is invalid. A great many people, including some at the upper rungs of the U.S. government, feel that since we have largely abandoned crusading against communism, the Soviets must somehow reciprocate by accommodating our interests. The fact is that this principle of reciprocity has never been acknowledged in Moscow; on the contrary, Soviet leaders have repeatedly stressed that detente does not mean an end to the struggle between the two political systems. They have expressed a desire to cooperate with the United States for the sake of peace in the world but it should be taken for granted that the Soviet idea of peace does not always coincide with ours, particularly in the areas where Soviet interests and security are at stake.

The Middle East

In both the United States and the Soviet Union, the Middle East has been considered a most difficult testing ground for detente. The hope for cooperation, however, may have been unrealistically high because the public has not appreciated the complexities of superpower interests in the area. Essentially, there has been the unalterable and comprehensive American commitment to Israel, matched—at least since 1955—by the Soviet political commitment to the Arab "anti-imperialist" cause in general, and to the support of Egypt and Syria against Israeli expansionism in particular. Because of these commitments, American and Soviet fortunes in the area have become a function of developments in the bitter Arab-Israeli conflict, with the risks of a direct confrontation constantly present. Thus the dangers of the situation would seem to dictate that the superpowers cooperate for the sake of peace and find ways of disengaging from their rigid commitments.

Such cooperation, however, has not been forthcoming because the U.S.-Soviet rivalry in the Middle East transcends the issue of the Arab-Israeli conflict. Even if this conflict were settled, the unique political, economic and strategic importance of the region excludes a possibility of one of them leaving the field free to the other to extend and strengthen its influence. This dual nature of their involvement in the area has determined a fundamental contradiction in the motives of the United States and the Soviet Union as they attempt to apply the spirit of detente to the Middle East. They are caught between an obvious need to avoid collision and to scale down the enormous costs of supporting the warring parties and the desire to pursue their own economic and strategic interests. While the first consideration calls for cooperation, the second accounts for a powerful impulse to seek out opportunities for undermining the rival's position. This impulse makes each side highly vulnerable to any setback or loss of prestige. It was inevitable, for example, that the discontinuation of diplomatic relations with the United States by a number of Arab states in the wake of the Six Day War in 1967 would be heralded as Soviet "victory." By the same token, the spectacular diplomatic comeback that Secretary of State Kissinger engineered following the October War of 1973 has been declared a "crushing defeat" for the Soviets.

An often underestimated aspect of detente in the Middle East is that while both superpowers are deeply involved there, neither can fully dominate the region. Aside from the vibrant nationalism of Israel and the Arab states, which are increasingly resisting excessive foreign influences, the fundamental incompatibility of communism and Islam, the economic ties of the oil-producing states to the West, and the continuing U.S. presence in the Mediterranean set limits to Soviet inroads. At the same time, the geographic proximity of the Soviet Union, with its consistent opposition to "neo-colonialist" practices, similarly restricts American freedom of action. Perhaps even more important is the unanimous resistance of our principal allies to any American actions which might result in a new embargo of Arab oil deliveries and threaten them with economic collapse. Finally, the American public, still remembering the lessons of Vietnam, would be unlikely to endorse foreign military ventures unless a devastating economic depression resulted in widespread despair and produced demands for "action."

These limitations do not prevent the superpowers from constant maneuvering in search of political and strategic advantages, from committing seemingly disproportionate diplomatic, military and economic means of pressure and inducement, and from engaging in actions which encourage further destabilization of the already volatile situation.

Acknowledging the inevitability of a continuing rivalry, the joint U.S.-Soviet communiqué, issued at the conclusion of President Nixon's visit to Moscow in 1972, made no reference to the broader problems of the Middle East or to possible ways of resolving them. Dealing with the Arab-Israeli conflict in the most general terms, the communiqué merely stated that the two governments "reaffirm their support for a peaceful settlement in the Middle East in accordance with Security Council Resolution 242 . . . and declare their readiness to play their part in bringing it about." No joint or coordinated action toward that end was envisioned, probably because the signatories knew their limitations.

Insofar as the Soviet leaders were concerned, their judgment was all that mattered. Actions of the United States, however, have been restricted by conflicting pressures of interest groups and popular perceptions as reflected in the press and in Congress. These perceptions are often at considerable variance with realities and the judgment of the administration. Among other things, the public tends to grossly overestimate the extent of influence the superpowers can exercise in dealing with their respective client states. Better informed people have known all along, for instance, that Israel, because of the strong political support it enjoys in the United States, has successfully resisted delegating responsibility for its national security to the United States and has proven to be relatively immune to pressures from Washington. Until the October War, however, the same better-informed people had failed to acknowledge that the Soviet Union has encountered analogous difficulties in dealing with *its* presumed client, Egypt, despite such episodes as the Egyptian expulsion of Soviet advisers in 1972. The lesson is worth learning.

Egypt's political turnabout and acceptance of Henry Kissinger's cease-fire proposal, executed despite its continuing dependence on Soviet arms, provides a spectacular proof that it is an independent actor and not a puppet of any superpower. This turnabout can only partially be attributed to the skills of Secretary of State Kissinger, who succeeded in convincing President Sadat of the United States's determination to press for a solution to the Arab-Israeli conflict as outlined in Security Council Resolution 242, and to Sadat's belief that because of Israel's dependence on it, the United States alone could redress Arab grievances. The major cause for Sadat's alienation from Moscow was the accumulation of irritants in Soviet-Egyptian relations, accentuated by the failure of the Soviet leadership to live up to its commitment to enforce the cease-fire line prescribed by the Security Council Resolution of 22 October 1973.

In an interview with the publisher of *Al-hawadith* in April 1974,[1] President Sadat discussed Egyptian-Soviet relations with considerable

---

[1] *Middle East and North Africa*, FBIS-MEA-74-85, 1 May 1974, pp. D4-D19. Events related to the October War have been dealt with by Marvin Kalb and Bernard Kalb in their book, *Kissinger* (Boston: Little, Brown and Co., 1974).

candor. He recounted how, in the summer of 1967, the Soviets reneged on their promise to deliver long-range fighter-bombers and assume responsibility for Egypt's air defenses against the overwhelming Israeli air force. In 1970, as the Israelis began their deep penetration raids, the Soviets sent SAM-3 missiles and trained Egyptian crews to operate them. But although they renewed their promise to send long-range fighter-bombers, later they again reneged. Simultaneously, they pressed Cairo to go along with the so-called Rogers initiative, which called for a reopening of the Suez Canal but with no provisions for a final settlement.

As Israel's refusal to cooperate halted progress on the Rogers initiative, Sadat—by then already president of Egypt—went to Moscow to renew his plea for offensive weapons, only to be told by Soviet leaders that planes could be sent only if they would be placed under direct Soviet command. We can guess that the Soviets were merely exercising self-restraint and were unwilling to encourage Egypt (and Syria) to attack, in part for fear of confrontation with the United States, and in part because of the low esteem in which they held the war-making capacity of the Arabs. To Moscow, its commitment to Egypt was limited, and the limits were to be determined by Soviet—not Egyptian—leadership. But to Sadat, as he said in the *Al-hawadith* interview, the suggestion that bombers would be under full control of Soviet officers and crews appeared an unbearable infringement upon Egypt's sovereignty. He concluded that the superpowers had conspired to freeze the status quo, abandoning the Arabs to their frustrations. After the Brezhnev-Nixon summit in July 1972, he expelled most of the Soviet technicians and military experts.[2]

Unfortunately this journalistic account, based on scores of interviews with American and Israeli diplomats and intelligence officers, cannot serve as a primary source, helpful as it is in establishing chronology of events. There are too many unattributed quotations and too many statements implying interrelation of actions without sufficient evidence that the actions were in fact interrelated to make the story into anything more than a plausible reconstruction. Some assertions are clearly unsupportable by evidence. One citation is sufficient to illustrate the point. "Under pressure from hard-liners who contended that Russia could have both the benefits of detente with the United States *and* war in the Middle East, Brezhnev decided to increase the flow of sophisticated military equipment to Egypt."

[2] Sadat's statements to *Al-hawadith* are fully consistent with those he made at the time of the expulsion of Soviet technicians to the Arab Socialist Union National Congress and to a group of Egyptian newspaper publishers (*Newsweek*, 7 August 1972). Sadat complained that he had been led on by the promises and excuses of Soviet officials, who were determined to deny Egypt offensive capability. For additional analysis, see E. R. F. Sheehan, "Why Sadat Packed off the Russians," *New York Times Magazine*, 6 August 1972.

This political setback notwithstanding, the Soviets maintained their commitment to Egypt and continued to ship military supplies, although in much smaller quantities than Sadat desired. In this same interview, Sadat pointed out that Moscow refused to supply advanced offensive weapons even when offered to be paid in cash out of funds contributed by Algeria. Sadat's suspicion that the Soviets were determined to forestall Egypt's attack on Israel—or, at the very least, to dissociate themselves from it—was reinforced. Anxious to assert Egypt's independence, two days before the attack was launched he ordered the remaining Soviets out of the country, "to deprive Israel of the blackmail trump card it was playing—its claim that it was fighting the Soviets and not the Arabs."

Soviet Ambassador Vinogradov shed some light on Moscow's actions during the October War while addressing a group of leading politicians and officials in Cairo, on the eve of his departure in April 1974.[3] Given the crisis in Soviet-Egyptian relations and the composition of his audience, Vinogradov can be assumed to have spoken with relative candor, if only to give credibility to the Soviet position. He revealed that Sadat gave him a two-day notice of the imminent 6 October attack. Informed of this development, Moscow replied without equivocation that "the war decision was an Egyptian decision and that the Soviet Union would fulfill its commitments and would support the Arab rights with all military, political, and economic means."[4]

In spite of this reaffirmation (and the steady shipments of military supplies), the Soviets displayed visible anxiety to end the fighting as quickly as possible. As Vinogradov has said, between 6 and 9 October, on instructions from Moscow, he informed Sadat three times that Syria had requested the Soviet government "to make

---

[3] Vinogradov's statement was published by Beirut's newspaper *As-Safir* on 16 April 1974. For the text, see *Middle East and North Africa*, FBIS-MEA-74-80, 24 April 1974. Its veracity has not been questioned by American intelligence analysts, and there were no subsequent rebuttals in the Egyptian press.

[4] Kalb and Kalb, *Kissinger*, p. 453, state that Sadat informed Brezhnev about the date of the attack on 22 September. They do not supply the source of their information. Galia Golan, writing in *Survival* (May-June 1974), says that "the Soviet Union knew in advance about the impending Egyptian and Syrian attacks on Israeli forces . . . , but there is still no certainty whether she was fully informed of, and party to, the actual preparations for the 1973 Middle East War." She adds that "the very hasty departure of Soviet dependents from Egypt and advisers from Syria just a few days before the outbreak of war does indicate that the Soviet Union was in the end aware at least of the proposed timing, but only at a very late date." A similar conclusion was reached by Alvin E. Rubinstein, "Moscow and Cairo: Currents of Influence," *Problems of Communism*, July-August 1974.

a quick move to obtain an international resolution providing for a cease-fire." Sadat rejected the suggestion and expressed the wish that Syria would stop these appeals; the Egyptian offensive was still under way and he wanted to seize the Sinai passes before a cease-fire. Vinogradov also said that Moscow warned Sadat on 10 October to speed up the offensive in view of heavy concentrations of Israeli forces on the Egyptian front. The advice was not heeded, Israel counterattacked, and had reached the Suez Canal by 16 October as Soviet Premier Kosygin arrived in Cairo. Even then, according to Vinogradov, Sadat resisted the idea of a cease-fire. According to Egyptian sources, he finally agreed to the initial Soviet contacts with the United States only after Kosygin assured him that the cease-fire would be enforced by both superpowers or, if need be, by the Soviet Union alone.

According to the seemingly authorized American version of the events, the Soviets had made such contacts, possibly unknown to Sadat, on 10 October, but got nowhere because of fierce objections by Israel, which was preparing for its counteroffensive.[5] The next Soviet move took place on 19 October as Brezhnev, doubtless appraised by his own experts of the impending collapse of Egypt's resistance, requested that Kissinger immediately come to Moscow for "urgent consultations on the Middle East." The next day a frantic appeal from Sadat to secure the cease-fire quickly confirmed Soviet estimates of the situation.

By 20 October, the urgent need to stop fighting was realized both in Washington and Moscow. The day before, President Nixon had asked Congress for $2.2 billion in emergency aid to Israel and the airlift of the military supplies from the United States was already in full swing. But at the same time, the Organization of Arab Oil Exporting Countries (OAPEC) adopted a policy of production cutbacks and selective embargo; the largest oil exporter, Saudi Arabia, declared its embargo just as Kissinger arrived in Moscow (and President Nixon fired Watergate Special Prosecutor Archibald Cox). Also on 20 October, earlier in the day, the Soviets put their three airborne divisions on alert, a fact duly monitored by U.S. intelligence.

According to the American story, Brezhnev and Kissinger, in lengthy meetings on 20 and 21 October, hammered out a joint tactic in securing a cease-fire resolution at the U.N. Security Council. Brezhnev won Sadat's agreement to direct talks with Israel (a *sine qua non* for the Israeli government) by reassuring him that "Russia

---

[5] Marvin Kalb and Bernard Kalb, "Twenty Days in October," *New York Times Magazine*, 23 June 1974.

would—if necessary, alone—guarantee the observance of the cease-fire." On 22 October, the Security Council unanimously called for a cease-fire with all forces in place, to take effect by not later than 6:52 p.m. Middle East time on the same day.

There are obvious gaps in the story but we can assume that the 22 October cease-fire line, agreed upon by Moscow, Washington, and Cairo, was unpalatable to Israel, which continued the offensive in the Golan Heights and the Sinai for two more days, seizing additional hundreds of square miles of territory on the west bank of the canal and cutting off Egypt's 3rd Army. We can also assume that Sadat held Moscow responsible for the failure to stop Israeli forces on the agreed-upon line, for on 24 October he urged Brezhnev and Nixon to send a joint Soviet-American force to police the Suez cease-fire.

The United States rejected this suggestion outright. Engaging in a power play of their own, the Soviets alerted four more of their airborne divisions and resumed the flights of their transport planes to Egypt and Syria which had ceased the day before. Simultaneously, Brezhnev radioed to Nixon that unless the United States would cooperate, "we should be faced with the necessity urgently to consider the question of taking appropriate steps unilaterally. Israel cannot be allowed to get away with the violations." [6]

No Soviet action in fact was taken, but on 25 October, President Nixon, on the advice of Kissinger, Schlesinger, and the chairman of the Joint Chiefs of Staff, Admiral Moorer, ordered a worldwide alert of U.S. strategic forces, including a maximum readiness of the airborne forces. The action was denounced in Moscow as an attempt at intimidation but, because of the heavy American pressure on Israel, the fighting in the Sinai had finally ended and the rest was left to politics and diplomacy.

We do not know the exact terms of the Brezhnev-Kissinger agreement of 21 October, which evidently was foiled by the continuing Israeli offensive. But we can surmise that Sadat's subsequent spectacular turnabout in accepting the Kissinger plan was caused by the Soviet acquiescence in the *fait accompli*. Frustrated with the Soviet Union and no doubt greatly encouraged by Kissinger, Sadat placed his bets on the United States, thereby causing Moscow acute diplomatic embarrassment. The Soviets quietly retaliated by stopping all the deliveries of weapons, spare parts and ammunition to Egypt, but abstained from expressing official disapproval of Sadat's actions. Soviet propaganda continued to reiterate the "justice" of the Arab

---

[6] Ibid.

cause and the Egyptian press reciprocated by abstaining from direct attacks on the Soviet Union. Egypt's economic and military realities could not easily be negated by Kissinger's promises.

How well did detente survive the strains arising from the October War? The Soviets tried to force the events by appearing ready to intervene and live up to their commitment to Sadat. In this they failed. The United States sounded several warnings to Moscow and in the end threatened it with a nuclear attack, though the threat was not very credible. The Soviets denounced this action as nuclear blackmail, but did so in a low key. They let Kissinger and his diplomacy dominate the scene in achieving the cease-fire, and did not obstruct his initiatives to bring about the separation of Arab and Israeli forces and create a U.N.-policed neutral zone between them. Having largely lost voice in Cairo, they retained influence in Damascus, warning the Syrians not to accept the cease-fire as a substitute for an ultimate solution of the conflict and urging them to insist that it was only a first step leading to implementation of Security Council Resolution 242. This "advice" made Kissinger's task more difficult, but the giving of it was strictly within the understanding of the Moscow accords. Soviet propaganda also consistently emphasized the unswerving Soviet support of the Arabs against Israel and its "imperialist" supporters; but propaganda, as Soviet leaders have repeatedly proclaimed, has been specifically exempt from detente understandings.

It is likely that in spite of the embarrassment of being temporarily pushed aside by the ubiquitous Kissinger, at least some Soviet leaders have come to view the U.S.-sponsored cease-fire with a degree of equanimity. There were rumors that Brezhnev and Grechko came under severe criticism by their Politburo colleagues for the attempt to flex muscle in ordering the airborne alert, but no signs that they suffered a political setback. The reason might be that despite their present predicament, the Soviets saw a number of compensating factors. First, they were relieved that they had not become militarily involved in the Arab-Israeli fighting, a prospect no one in Moscow welcomed. Second, they can now draw satisfaction that Soviet prestige is in no direct way committed to the cease-fire arrangement which, especially in the Syrian case, they can rightly regard as rather fragile. Third, taking a long view, the Soviets can anticipate that Israeli intransigence and accompanying Arab frustrations may lead in time to yet another blowup and a new shift of alignments; the explosive and intractable Palestinian Arab problem, which has surfaced in United Nations forums, and the question of the status of Jerusalem promise to be particularly unmanageable.

In the meantime, the Soviets see some immediate opportunities which they can be expected to exploit, however carefully. American sales of advanced weapons to conservative Arab governments eliminate much of the rationale for Soviet self-restraint in this regard. Syria, Iraq, and perhaps Libya would be able to count on a greater understanding of their defense needs than Egypt could prior to the October War. Syria has received medium-range, ground-to-ground missiles; Iraq has even been reported to be receiving direct Soviet military support in its efforts to subdue the Kurdish rebellion.[7] This military assistance approach appears less promising in relations with Egypt as Sadat tries to diminish his dependence on Soviet military aid by purchasing advanced weapons in Western Europe. Yet the fact remains that Egypt's armed forces are in large measure Soviet-equipped and are constantly in need of spare parts and ammunition which are obtainable only in the U.S.S.R. It can be assumed that this dependence, despite Sadat's arms arrangements with the French, would continue to give the Soviet Union a degree of influence on Cairo's policies. Finally, the weapons the Soviets sell these days to Arabs are paid for in hard currency supplied by oil-rich countries, constituting a sizeable source of revenue to the Soviet treasury.

On the diplomatic front, a staunch Soviet (and Chinese) backing of the interests of 1.5 million Palestinian Arabs, whose fate practically every Middle Eastern country had until recently ignored, could measurably complicate United States mediation efforts. Since Kissinger is most unlikely to resolve the conflict singlehandedly, the Soviets would eventually have their say at the Geneva Conference—when and if it reconvenes—which they cosponsored with the United States. The American hand, however, has been very much weakened by the U.N. General Assembly's invitation to Yasser Arafat to address its forum; and particularly by the Arab decision (at the Rabat Conference in October 1974) to recognize the PLO as the sole representative of the Palestinians. As for the Soviets, they found the most intriguing of all the Middle East developments to be the entirely unexpected oil embargo declared in October 1973, which demonstrated the power of the Arab states to affect the whole well-being of the Western world.

Oil Embargo

The spectacular action of the Organization of Arab Petroleum Exporting Countries (OAPEC) which, at the height of the Middle East crisis,

---

[7] *Washington Post*, 5 October 1974.

announced a cutback of oil production and embargo on the shipments of oil to the countries that sided with Israel in the October War (the United States, Holland, Portugal, and South Africa) introduced an entirely new factor into world politics. The action was preceded and accompanied by enormous increases in the prices of oil which damaged the economic well-being of the advanced industrial nations and upset established patterns of international trade. Some argue that the price hikes would have occurred in any case, with countries like Iran, Iraq, Venezuela, or Algeria needing additional funds for their economic development. It is undeniable, however, that the October War served as a catalyst for a joint and well-coordinated action without which the prices would not have gone up as high and as fast as they did, and the embargo would not have been instituted.

In a narrow sense, the oil embargo episode lies outside the scope of Soviet-American detente analysis. It might have been, of course, that in many of his conversations with President Sadat, Ambassador Vinogradov discussed various ways and means of applying pressure on supporters of Israel, including a utilization of the "oil weapon."[8] It is equally likely that Sadat was able to consider this on his own and did not need anybody's coaching. Moreover, Sadat's principal link to the oil-producing states was through the late King Faisal of Saudi Arabia and he knew that Faisal's price for this kind of cooperation was a weakening of the Egyptian-Soviet tie. It can safely be assumed that Vinogradov and his superiors in Moscow were aware of this, and, for this reason, could not be particularly enthusiastic about this prospect.[9]

Once the oil embargo was announced, many public figures and political writers in the United States began to voice suspicion that the Soviets either instigated or in some mysterious way influenced the OAPEC decision. In the absence of any evidence supporting them, these speculations cannot be considered seriously. Most of the oil-producing states have had no relations with the Soviet Union and

---

[8] For about a year before the October War, Radio Moscow in Arabic had been urging utilization of the "oil weapon" in the struggle against imperialism. Although there is no evidence that the oil embargo was declared because of Soviet prodding, the latter is still indicative of consistency of long-term Communist objectives. For citations and analysis, see Foy D. Kohler, Leon Goure and Mose L. Harvey, *The Soviet Union and the October 1973 Middle East War: The Implications for Detente* (Center for Advanced International Studies, University of Miami, 1974), pp. 80-83.

[9] The late King Faisal's militant anticommunism and Saudi links with "international oil monopolies," along with Sadat's heavy dependence on the king's generosity, ought to have ruled out Soviet hopes that a Saudi-Egyptian link would result in a militantly anti-U.S. posture of Saudi Arabia.

in their politics have been openly hostile to communism in any shape or form. Iraq, which stands the closest to Moscow because of frictions with Iran and because of the vexing Kurdish problem, not only refused to join OAPEC in its embargo but actually increased its production of oil, selling it to the highest bidders without discrimination.

Even if they had little to do with the embargo, however, the Soviets have paid their utmost attention to the emergence of OAPEC as a new "anti-imperialist" force in world politics.[10] Communist propaganda hailed the OAPEC action as signifying an end to the "unconscionable exploitation" of Arab natural resources by the multinational oil corporations. The violent anticommunism of the Arabs has been ignored as if it were irrelevant to the Soviet position and OAPEC dependence on Western markets was played down. The prospect of economic decline in advanced industrial nations resulting from the high costs of fuel appeared equally irrelevant to immediate Soviet interests, although Western observers could argue that the inevitable inflation in the West promised to make the goods Moscow wanted to import, and the credits needed to pay for them, much more costly.

These developments suggest several observations. First, although the Soviets have acknowledged the link between the OAPEC action and the Arab-Israeli conflict, and praised Arab solidarity, Communist propaganda has avoided emphasizing these aspects, probably anticipating their temporary nature. Second, the Soviet endorsement of OAPEC has demonstrated that a weakening of the "imperialist camp" still occupies a dominant place on the list of Moscow's foreign policy objectives. The current uncertainties of detente and the plain fact of the emergence of the "oil weapon" as a factor in international politics and economics only enhance the importance of this stand. Third, in taking a firm pro-OAPEC position and in emphasizing the question of Palestinian Arabs, the Soviets attain a twin goal: they compensate themselves to some extent for the diplomatic setback incurred as the United States actively reentered the Arab world and, at the same time, by opposing the oil-consuming nations, they reassert their ideological purity, in the process heading off Peking's attempts to become the foremost champion of Third World and "national-liberation" causes.

A fourth point, of much greater significance from the Soviet point of view, has been a sudden and dramatic cleavage between the United States on the one hand and its principal allies in Europe and

---

[10] See, for instance, R. Andreasyan, "Neft' i antimperialisticheskaya bor'ba" [Oil and anti-imperialist struggle], *Kommunist*, no. 5 (1974).

Asia on the other. Even as the fighting in the Middle East was raging in October, the NATO allies (save for Portugal and Greece) refused to cooperate in the massive American supply of military equipment to Israel by denying use of their airfields for landing and refueling of the American transport planes and by vetoing the transshipments of materiel the United States had committed to NATO. The fear of Arab retaliation, with its threat to their economic wellbeing, became so overwhelming that all major NATO powers (and Japan) unequivocally disassociated themselves from American pro-Israeli policies and categorically refused to take part in any joint action Washington wanted to initiate against the Arab oil cartel. In the scramble for securing oil supplies for their economies, it was every nation for itself, vividly demonstrating the narrowness of the limits of allied cooperation.

Menacing speeches and editorials in the United States, and the dark hints that a lack of allied cooperation in the Middle East might lead to a reconsideration of the American security commitments, only irritated the allies. Their response, in effect, was that if forced to choose between a long-term Soviet strategic threat without the benefit of the American nuclear umbrella, and a prospect of an imminent economic collapse, they would clearly accept the former. Not only did the allies express disapproval of the open-ended United States commitment to Israel, they voiced stern warnings that they would not acquiesce in any application of force or other forms of coercion to bend the Arab will.

This unprecedented isolation of the United States from its closest friends was duly noted in Moscow. Almost equally significant to the Soviets appeared the courage with which weak Arab states withstood the fury of American indignation over the oil embargo and the spectacular price increases; even the geographically most exposed and determinedly anti-Communist Iran openly warned Washington not to undertake any foolish schemes.

These developments were appreciated in Washington as well, giving a powerful boost to Kissinger's efforts aimed at winning over the Arabs even at the cost of infuriating the Jewish community. Yet, on their part, the Soviets could claim a share of credit for making the joint Arab stand possible. Without expecting a political reorientation of the oil-producing states (and realistically assessing their interdependence with Western oil consumers), the Soviets are satisfied that their geographic proximity to the Middle East and their stated opposition to "neo-colonialism" have helped to discourage those who may have otherwise considered resolving the oil crisis by the methods of "gunboat diplomacy." Kissinger's statement (in the interview with *Business Week* given on 23 December 1974) that the United States might resort to military action if there were "some actual strangulation of the industrialized world" evoked a strongly negative reaction in Moscow. *Pravda*'s political observer stated in the issue of 18 January 1975:

> Rejecting a policy of blackmail, threats, and intimidation resorted to by U.S. ruling circles which use the pretext of "defense of the West," both the Soviet and international public declare that such a policy sharply contradicts the tendency implicit in détente, in developing inter-state relations according to principles of equality and cooperation.

Although this is essentially a political stand, committing the Soviet Union to no particular action, it is also an indication that the Soviets continually reexamine their detente policies, probably questioning some of their earlier premises. A probability of severe economic dislocations in the West because of quadrupled oil prices requires significant changes in the foreign trade planning of the Soviet Union. The dramatically demonstrated failure of the United States to develop a common policy with its allies vis-à-vis the oil-producing nations calls for an overall reassessment of American power, with important implications for Soviet security. Intense studies of the changing strategic picture, reported to be under way in Moscow, are aimed at determining the various political, military, economic and diplomatic options which can be made available to the Soviet Union as detente continues to evolve. There might be new opportunities in Third World countries upon which the West depends for critical minerals, new inducements to Japan and other nations to invest more heavily into the development of Russia's natural resources, and new possibilities for exploiting frictions within NATO and the Common Market, to maximize Soviet interests. Such a reappraisal is a cumbersome process under the Soviet system, and some time would elapse before decisions would take place. One can guess, however, that in the absence of Soviet goodwill the going promises to be rougher for the United States than in the past.

The Cyprus Crisis

The military takeover in Cyprus in July 1974 had nothing to do with the U.S.-Soviet detente. Archbishop Makarios was mildly favored in Moscow for his nonalignment policy and mildly detested in Washington for the same. His principal opponents were in the Cypriote

National Guard, directed by Greek officers dedicated to the cause of enosis, that is, union with Greece, and opposed to giving autonomy to the Turkish minority in Cyprus. On signal from Athens, they staged a coup d'etat and proclaimed a military regime which lasted only a few days, collapsing as soon as Turkey invaded the island.

The task of the United States was to localize the crisis and prevent a confrontation reminiscent of those of 1964 and 1967 between NATO allies, Greece and Turkey, and, if possible, to forestall a Turkish invasion of Cyprus. The first task was accomplished because of the political and military weakness of Greece, which was unable to challenge Turkey. The Athens junta fell apart at the height of the crisis, paving the way for restoration of a civilian government. A widespread public approval for this latter development did not alter Kissinger's disposition to "tilt" toward Turkey, which he considered more valuable to NATO than Greece.[11] The internal weaknesses of the Turkish government impelled Kissinger to acquiesce in Ankara's actions. The consequences were dramatic and far-reaching, internationally as well as domestically. The U.S. offer to mediate the Greek-Turkish-Cypriote conflict was repeatedly rebuffed, and the Karamanlis government announced withdrawal of the Greek forces from NATO. In the aftermath, the United States incurred the lasting wrath of the Greeks without gaining the sympathy of the Turks or appreciation for its self-restraint among its European allies. Kissinger was roundly accused of a callousness bordering on immorality for allowing a de facto partitioning of the island and a dissolution of the Republic of Cyprus to take place.[12]

The Soviets were initially caught between their stated dedication to independence of Cyprus and a pragmatic need to cultivate friendly relations with Turkey which, until the advent of Karamanlis in Greece, they had regarded as the weakest link in the NATO alliance in the Mediterranean area. The change of government in Athens opened new opportunities for exploiting the wave of anti-American sentiment sweeping Greece. In these circumstances, the Soviets chose to do nothing; they righteously blamed the tragedy of Cyprus on "NATO machinations" rather than on the Greeks or the Turks and demanded the "withdrawal of foreign troops from its soil,"

---

[11] Rowland Evans and Robert Novak, "Paying the Price of Neglecting Turkey," *Washington Post*, 17 August 1974; Tom Braden, "Secretary Kissinger and Cyprus," *Washington Post*, 30 August 1974.

[12] See Richard Holbrooke, "Henry Kissinger," *Washington Post*, 15 September 1974.

which meant the closing of the two British military bases on the island as much as the withdrawal of Turkish occupation forces.[13]

Having adopted a hands-off attitude, fully compatible with the spirit of detente, the Soviets could bide their time, watch the discomfiture of the United States, and hope, not without reason, that the British would liquidate their military presence in Cyprus. The Soviets anticipate an additional buildup of tensions in Greece and in Turkey, as well as in the relations between them, and count on a further decline of American power and influence in the Mediterranean and in the NATO alliance.

Europe

Since the conclusion of the Quadripartite Agreement on West Berlin in September 1971, which has successfully removed a major stumbling block in improvement of East-West relations, and the establishment of diplomatic relations between the United States and the German Democratic Republic, little has happened in Europe which could properly be considered as falling within the context of the U.S.-Soviet detente. In theory, there is room for cooperation on the issue of mutual force reduction (MFR), but this has become hopelessly entangled in problems of interallied relationships in NATO. There is a widespread apprehension that in the present political climate any major alteration in the existing set-up might badly shake the whole edifice of NATO, and a prospect of reducing forces in negotiations with the enemy before some acceptable new strategy had been worked out within the alliance does not appeal to anyone. France, in keeping with its principle that national security cannot be delegated to any international body or rest on any international agreement, does not even participate in MFR talks.

Soviet interest in MFR has been marginal from the beginning, and Moscow accepted the idea of linking it with the Conference on Security and Cooperation in Europe (CSCE) only at Washington's insistence. This American position had little relation to the American objectives with regard to reducing tensions in Europe, but had a great deal to do with congressional pressure to cut back U.S. forces there, unilaterally if necessary. So long as the MFR talks continue, the administration can argue in favor of maintaining a strong bargaining position, such as keeping U.S. forces in Europe on the present level.

---

[13] Address by Soviet Foreign Minister A. A. Gromyko before the U.N. General Assembly, 19 September 1974. Also, Peter Osnos, "Soviet Seek to Balance Interests in Policy on Cyprus," *Washington Post*, 24 August 1974.

MFR talks have contributed little to relaxation of tensions in the heart of Europe. From the beginning, each side has been apprehensive lest an MFR agreement would result in its relative disadvantage vis-à-vis the opposing bloc. Thus it has been all but inevitable that one side would knowingly advance proposals that the other side would find unacceptable. Such a tactic has resulted in a virtual freeze in the negotiating positions, reducing the benefits of the conference to its not insignificant educational value. In spite of the pretense that the conference participants represent their individual sovereign interests, nobody has ever doubted that these have in fact been negotiations between NATO and the Warsaw Pact, requiring close coordination of positions within each alliance. The issues discussed in Vienna have not commanded high-level attention either in Moscow or in Washington but the conference has served the unstated purposes of both: rather than diminishing the cohesion of the two security systems, the negotiations helped to solidify them, perhaps more in the case of NATO than the Warsaw Pact.

The CSCE talks, for which the Soviet Union had pressed for years, succeeding in evoking some public support in Western Europe, have degenerated into a general exercise in public relations. Being only one of thirty-five participants, the United States has had limited influence on CSCE deliberations; even the Soviet Union has had difficulties in coordinating the positions of its East European allies. Certain areas of general agreement have been outlined: economic cooperation, scientific-cultural exchanges, and even the somewhat touchy subject of the inviolability of existing frontiers. Disturbing to the Soviet Union, however, has been a surprisingly unanimous demand of non-Communist states (viewed with a degree of sympathy also by Yugoslavia and Poland) that if Europe is to be regarded as one entity, there ought to be tangible progress towards obtaining a freer flow of ideas, people, and information across what once had been described as the iron curtain. The Soviet view that the concept of "one Europe" should in no way diminish the sovereign right of each government to regulate such movements has been rejected by a majority of participants.[14] Since Moscow feels that relinquishing this right would open the way for all sorts of subversive influences in its domain, the issue has become a stumbling block at CSCE with no immediate prospects of overcoming it.

---

[14] See Gromyko, U.N. address. On Soviet military plans in Europe, see Thomas W. Wolfe, *Soviet Military Capabilities and Intentions in Europe* (Santa Monica, Calif.: The Rand Corporation, March 1974). On CSCE, see Mojmir Povolny, "The Soviet Union and the European Security Conference," *Orbis*, Spring 1974.

While knowing that it is unacceptable to the Soviets, the United States has supported this demand for cultural freedom throughout Europe. But it would require a considerable stretch of imagination for the Soviet leaders to ascribe difficulties they experience solely to American plotting and intrigue. It is likely, therefore, that CSCE will be kept outside U.S.-Soviet detente relations, and that Moscow will continue to deal with individual European nations much as before. In this case, Soviet expectations from the CSCE exercise would probably be scaled down. At the same time, original fears in the West that CSCE would erode Western unity (whatever that may mean) are also likely to be put to rest and, as in the case of MFR, this continuing conference would most likely occupy a minor place in the total foreign endeavors of the United States.

The China Factor

The governments of the United States and the Soviet Union would vigorously deny the suggestion that the improvement of American relations with the People's Republic of China could be considered detrimental to Soviet-American detente. At the same time, there are few who doubt that the dramatic reversal of Sino-American relations in 1971–72 has been an important factor in detente developments. On the one hand, it has put an end to popular conception of a threatening Communist monolith, thereby diminishing the sense of mission in United States foreign policy. On the other, if this can be considered a loss, it has been amply compensated, in the eyes of the government, by the emergence of a new and disturbing dimension to Soviet security needs posed by the U.S.-P.R.C. rapprochement.

With the passage of time, however, the China factor seems to have lost some of its initial significance. Although trade has been expanding rapidly, relations with China have not warmed up to the extent originally hoped for, and any capacity in Washington for influencing Peking's policy has materialized only marginally. The P.R.C. is still viewed as a potential menace to some American allies in Asia, and keeping this menace potential rather than active remains a primary U.S. policy objective.

In the context of U.S.-Soviet detente, the China factor also appears to have become less immediate. Peking's hopes—if such have been entertained—of influencing Washington in the direction of a harder anti-Soviet line, have not been realized; the last thing the United States wants is additional tensions with the Soviets. At the same time, in areas of major American concern, such as Europe or the Middle East, the P.R.C. can do little either to help or to hurt.

The Sino-Soviet conflict, in spite of recurring jitters that it might flare up and get out of control, is still considered in Washington to be a positive phenomenon in so far as it absorbs the attention and energies of the two Communist giants. But it appears that lately the Soviets have become less preoccupied with the Yellow Peril. Never believers in give-and-take in dealing with an enemy, they have amassed impressive military forces along the border with China. Apparently intimidated by this display, the Chinese have been practicing restraint and avoiding incidents which could provoke a massive Soviet retaliation. This has confirmed to Moscow leaders the validity of their tactic. But at the same time, leaders in Peking have also begun to sound less alarmed, repeatedly stating to visiting foreigners that the danger of Soviet attack on China has passed.[15]

Yet the China factor does have influence upon U.S.-Soviet detente. The Chinese may have determined that a greater American influence in Moscow provides a modicum of deterrent to possible Soviet moves against the P.R.C. To the Soviets, a possibility of a U.S.-Chinese collusion (if not alliance) against the Soviet Union has become an integral part of the overall strategic picture, permanently affecting their diplomacy and military planning. After a rebuffed attempt during SALT I negotiations to evolve a coordinated position for a hypothetical case of Chinese nuclear misbehavior, the Soviets have not brought the subject up again, apparently having concluded that they ought to be prepared to deal singlehandedly should such a danger arise.[16] While trying to normalize state-to-state relations with the P.R.C. by continuing negotiation of the border disputes and improvement of trade relations, the Soviets keep careful watch over any international moves by Peking which could be inimical to their interests, counteracting them wherever they can by their own maneuvers.

It would be a considerable error to conclude, however, that the Soviets regard the United States and the P.R.C. as belonging to the same category of Soviet enemies. In doctrinal-political terms which, after all, still determine the general direction of Soviet leaders' thinking, the idea of U.S.-Soviet "convergence" remains anathema while China's present behavior is not seen as precluding Sino-Soviet rapprochement at some future date. As one authoritative source puts it,

---

[15] John Burns, "Peking Says Soviet Threat Has Eased," *Washington Post*, 5 October 1974.

[16] John Newhouse, *Cold Dawn* (New York: Holt, Rinehart and Winston, 1973), p. 176.

> No country should be "excommunicated" from socialism just on the basis of certain ideological or political differences. Disagreements on separate questions . . . *if they do not lead to attempts to restore bourgeois social relations or to an actual alliance of a particular country with the imperialist powers against the other socialist countries* [italics added], do not put any socialist state outside the world socialist system.[17]

Thus, so long as the P.R.C. remains socialist and avoids allying itself with the United States against the Soviet Union, its anti-Soviet posture would be seen in Moscow qualitatively different from that of "American imperialism" even if at the moment it may appear to pose a greater menace to the Soviet Union.

Looking at the situation in the context of Soviet-American detente, it should be concluded that the China factor is much more a matter of pragmatic preoccupation for the Soviet political and national security establishments than a function of the triangular relationship involving the United States. Thus it can be expected that Moscow would remain alert to opportunities to exacerbate U.S.-Chinese relations, while Peking would not miss a chance to do the same to U.S.-Soviet relations. The fundamental fact remains, however, that each of the three protagonists is essentially immune to political manipulation and military pressures of the others and is distinctly unwilling to pursue any interests except its own.

---

[17] A. Butenko, ed., *The World Socialist System and Anticommunism* (Moscow: Progress Publishers, 1972), English edition, pp. 135-36.

3
PROSPECTS FOR DETENTE

Foreign policy of the Soviet Union is determined by a combination of internal needs, external opportunities, and a sense of purpose arising from a value system known as Communist ideology. In the post-Khrushchev years, as more and more people and institutions became involved in the formation of foreign policy, this process has become increasingly more complex and cumbersome. While the ultimate decisions on specific matters are still made by the Politburo (with a more or less perfunctory approval by the plenums of the Central Committee of the Communist Party of the Soviet Union [CC CPSU]), preparation of these decisions, requiring consensus of interested government agencies and CC CPSU departments, takes a great deal of time and deliberation.

Once a major policy—such as the pursuit of detente with the United States and other countries of the "imperialist camp"—is adopted, its guidelines become mandatory for all, consistently reflected in the news media and official statements. As internal conditions and external circumstances related to the policy change, the appropriate offices and institutions reexamine the premises upon which it is based. This reexamination, however, takes place behind closed doors, only infrequently finding reflection in specialized journals or ambiguous passages in newspaper articles. The public is ignorant of the changes unless and until the Politburo decides that there is enough justification for a substantial modification, or even a reversal of the policy.[1]

The guidelines for U.S.-Soviet detente relations are contained in a document entitled "Basic Principles of Relations between the United

---

[1] For a more detailed discussion of the subject, see V. Petrov, "Formation of Soviet Foreign Policy," *Orbis*, Fall 1973.

47

States of America and the Union of Soviet Socialist Republics" (see Appendix) which had been approved by the Politburo and was signed by Brezhnev and Nixon on 29 May 1972. We do not know what the actual expectations of the Soviet leaders were at that time. It is possible that the accomplishments of the succeeding years have exceeded their expectations, but it is equally possible, indeed likely, that since the high point in the fall of 1972, many developments have proved disappointing. On the whole, however, the Soviets have maintained an optimistic view; at the time of President Nixon's visit to Moscow in July 1974, the populace was repeatedly advised that detente was "irreversible," that the American enemies of detente, influential as they might be, could not turn back the clock of history. No doubt there is skepticism, soul-searching, and reappraisal of particular policies and diplomatic tactics taking place in councils of the CC CPSU and in the Soviet government. But these will be effectively barred from public view until the final synthesis has been made at the very top. The Politburo and the Secretariat of the Central Committee, which form the ruling Soviet consensus, must determine and announce any changes in the direction of policy.

Decisive for the future of U.S.-Soviet detente is the leadership's perception of the world at large, of Soviet and American roles in it, and of the internal political scene in the United States. Appraising the latter, the Soviets are as much concerned with the general atmosphere as they are with specific accomplishments and failures in Soviet-American relations. This concern needs to be appreciated, for in spite of a remarkable growth of Soviet power in recent decades, one still detects a pervasive sense of inferiority in Moscow, which has deep psychological and historical roots. Neither economic difficulties in the United States, nor the erosion of the power of the presidency, nor the rather spectacular decline of America's international influence have so far provided sufficient reassurance to the Soviet leaders who are only too well aware that the Soviet Union itself is not exactly a showcase of prosperity, and that its own international following is neither impressive nor reliable.

The main Soviet motivation in embarking on a policy of reducing international tensions with "imperialist" powers was to create conditions under which material resources and national energies could be redirected from the wasteful defense effort and politically motivated foreign aid toward more constructive goals of building the economic might of Russia and raising the standard of living of its populace. Such redirection, however, could take place only if there were no corresponding weakening of the relative physical security of the Soviet Union and its allies or the ability to derive prestige and political benefits from military power. In Soviet judgment and in American judgment as well, a substantial degree of mutual trust between the superpowers must precede substantive agreements on such matters as strategic arms limitation and disarmament, force reductions in Europe, naval rivalry in the Mediterranean and the Indian Ocean, or sales of weapons to friendly nations. Since such a degree of trust has not been achieved, the U.S.-Soviet negotiations have largely become exercises in diplomatic maneuvering where the principal goal is to attain advantage over the adversary.

From the Soviet point of view, the movement in the direction of general relaxation can become irreversible only if there is a consistent pro-detente sentiment in both countries. The Soviets claim they have succeeded in creating such sentiment in their country. Professional observers of Soviet affairs know that propagandistic denunciations of American "imperialism" notwithstanding, the Soviets in recent years have been reasonably consistent in stressing positive aspects of Soviet-American relations; their critique of the American society has been toned down markedly. There are, of course, influential people in Moscow who have strong reservations about detente, but the effectively controlled news media does not permit expressions of such sentiments to challenge the official policy.

Such is not, in the Soviet view, the situation in the United States, where detente policies of the Nixon and Ford administrations have been under continuous fire. As they survey the American political scene, the Soviets see a number of forces opposing improvement of relations with the Soviet Union: the notorious "military-industrial complex," with the Pentagon as its principal stronghold; elements in the federal bureaucracy psychologically tied to their cold war antecedents; old-line anti-Communist organizations and movements reinvigorated by agitation of recent refugees from communism; the AFL-CIO which opposes expansion of trade with the Soviet Union, in part because of its protectionist disposition, but in large measure due to its ingrained anticommunism; and an influential segment of the news media, so detested by the Soviets for its messianic spirit and constant efforts to prod them toward "liberalization."

Above all, the Soviets watch with constant alarm activities of the so-called "Zionist circles" which considerably overlap, in their judgment, the categories of enemies listed above. By this, they mean leaders and members of the American Jewish community which turned decidedly anti-Soviet in the late 1960s. Moscow sees this change not merely as a result of the Soviet Union's pro-Arab stand in the Middle East (many Western countries, including some of the United States's closest allies take a pro-Arab position), but also, and perhaps primarily, as a reaction to the decline of Jewish influence in the Soviet Union.

This is a very touchy subject these days, rarely elaborated in print or public speeches. The Soviets concede that after many years of preeminent influence in political, administrative, economic and cultural affairs of Russia, Jews have been compelled to make room for other nationalities. The Soviets hotly deny, however, though not very convincingly to outside observers, that this process has been stimulated and accompanied by Russian, Ukrainian, or Byelorussian anti-Semitism; they point out that the continuing prominence of Jews in many important fields of Soviet life is still greatly disproportionate to their numbers in the population as a whole. (The Soviets refuse to recognize the elementary and sociologically proven fact that discrimination can manifest itself not only in the denial of rights and opportunities to a given group but also in a partial loss of that group's once privileged positions to other competing groups.)

As they indignantly react to charges of anti-Semitism (and stress the need for a "balance" in their multinational country), the Soviets suspect American Jews of constantly plotting against Soviet interests in general, against the administration's policy of normalizing relations with the Soviet Union, and against a reduction of tensions in the explosive Middle East. The latter activity baffles and worries them. According to Soviet analysis, an improvement in American relations with the Arabs is crucial for the American economy and the preservation of American alliances; therefore the ability of the Jewish community to inhibit this improvement proves to Moscow its enormous political power quite out of proportion to its numerical size.[2] It is because of this power that the Soviets regard Jewish participation in fomenting anti-Soviet sentiments in the United States with utmost concern. They perceive it as almost hopeless to try to neutralize Jewish hostility by the limited acts of goodwill which they consider feasible within their own political context, expecting relentless pressure for more and more concessions.

Somewhat belatedly, the Soviets came to appreciate the paralyzing effect of the Watergate scandal in the Nixon administration and to understand the multiplicity of motivations behind the anti-Nixon campaign. They nevertheless believe that the campaign was

---

[2] The Gallup Poll, reported in the *Washington Post* on 26 January 1975, indicated that less than 9 percent of the respondents favored any kind of aid to Israel, a fact duly noted by Soviet-U.S. watchers.

to a large extent generated by the powerful anti-Soviet forces accusing the administration of yielding too much to Russia, of betraying the cherished American ideals of freedom and democracy to the foremost enemy in its callousness to the predicament of Soviet Jews, of compromising American economic interests and defense posture, and of not being tough enough in dealing with the Arabs.

These charges sounded strange to the Soviets. They had credited the Nixon administration with certain innovations in style and form, but respected it primarily for its realization of the limits of American power and willingness to discontinue the cold war rhetoric.[3] They welcomed continuous top-level communications and appreciated manifestations of social acceptability accorded to them in meetings with American leaders. And they valued an opportunity to have access to American markets, particularly to advanced technology and agricultural commodities. But at no time did they believe that establishment of better relations with the Soviet Union had become a principal objective of the Nixon administration, superseding the natural "imperialist" urge to manipulate Soviet behavior to American advantage and to hurt Soviet interests wherever possible. Examples were manifest: the opening to China, the mining of the Haiphong harbor on the eve of Nixon's visit to Moscow, the continued funding of anti-Soviet undertakings (such as Radio Liberty), the constant efforts of Kissinger to outmaneuver the Soviet Union politically and diplomatically, the attempts to extend American influence to Eastern Europe, the meddling into Soviet internal affairs in the name of "human rights," the periodic flexing of the American military muscle for political advantages—all these policies have provided the Soviets with abundant proof that detente, to the United States, no less than to the Soviet Union, has been a very limited proposition, in no sense eliminating their adversary relationship. Based entirely on self-interest, it has been merely a step in the right direction.

Given this not unrealistic Soviet perception of the Nixon-Kissinger view of detente, the frontal attack against the administration for being, in effect, "soft on the Soviets" has been gravely disturbing to Soviet leaders as auguring a new era of tensions, of acceleration of the arms race, and of confrontations reminiscent of the cold war. While the Nixon administration appeared salvageable, the Soviet press stressed the positive, and Soviet detente rhetoric differed little from that of American officials. With the demise of Nixon and

---

[3] See analysis by V. Zhurkin, "Razryadka i mezhdunarodnyie konflikty" [Detente and international conflicts], *Mezhdunarodnaya zhizn'* [International life], no. 6 (1974).

a sharper questioning of Kissinger's actions (no doubt privately ascribed in Moscow, at least in part, to his "tilting" towards the Arabs after the October War), the Soviets had to reassess the situation. Witnessing the ascent on the political scene of the more militantly anti-Soviet forces, usually identified with Senator Henry M. Jackson, they stopped talking about "irreversibility of detente" and began to appeal instead for "creating conditions which would eventually make detente irreversible"—a subtle but most important change. Compelled to explain to domestic critics of detente [4] the adverse developments in the United States, they also felt the need to stress Soviet gains. As the deputy chief of the CC CPSU International Department, V. V. Zagladin, stated recently,

> detente is a product of a multifaceted class struggle . . . of two opposing systems in the world arena; it is also a struggle in which all revolutionary forces participate [because] detente creates new and most favorable conditions for the developing fight for democracy and socialism.

It is for this reason, warns Zagladin, that "the most aggressive imperialist forces resist detente," both internationally and within their respective societies, and he underscores that "the growth of anticommunism in the capitalist world is a convincing proof of activation of the forces of the Right." [5]

This kind of hedging has in it all the trappings of an ideological retrenchment, paving the way for a policy change if developments (such as an improvement of Senator Jackson's chances to be elected President in 1976) so warrant. To Moscow watchers it is a good evidence that Soviet leaders are searching for policy alternatives to be exercised if the political climate in the United States deteriorates further and the administration is rendered helpless to pursue detente with any kind of vigor. The most obvious decision would be to take an uncompromising defense posture, forcing greater defense outlays upon the United States. Another would be a more militant agitation against American "imperialism," contributing to an increase of tensions in international relations. Finally, Moscow may decide to work more diligently than in recent years against American interests in Europe, in the Middle East, and in parts of Asia and Africa.

This is all possible. Yet it is doubtful that the Soviets would raise the level of conflict to a point where they would endanger

---

[4] Of course, we do not know who, exactly, these critics are. Their categorization by Roy Medvedev, prominent Soviet dissident (*Washington Post*, 8 October 1974), is as good as any.
[5] Zagladin, "Along the New Historical Path," pp. 12-14.

advantages already accomplished as a result of the U.S.-Soviet detente relationship. They also probably know that their ability to hurt American interests is limited, and even if they chose to exercise it, a decline for the United States would help little in resolving Russia's own problems.

As the Soviets see it, a lack of American cooperation in the economic field may delay an improvement of the standard of living in Russia by a few years, but in the primary area of military technology they have been relying on their own resources all along. The more liberal elements in Moscow are probably more concerned that a failure of detente would mean a greater role for political conservatives in the Soviet bureaucracy, resulting in less freedom in cultural affairs, in reduced communications with the outside world, and in a general "neo-Stalinist" trend whose manifestations few venture to predict.[6]

Soviet international politics, however, are unlikely to acquire a new revolutionary dynamism. There have been too many adverse developments abroad, from the counter-revolution in Chile to the "defection" of Egypt—to cite two recent examples—for the Soviets to be overly optimistic about what they can accomplish. Relations with China remain a sore point, and the Warsaw Pact Organization and COMECON do not seem to display much vitality. Thus Soviet hopes for improvement of their international posture would seem to rest more on the relative decline of the West rather than on the appeal of communism, or of the Soviet political system, to other societies. Moscow might be tempted to contribute to this decline, but playing upon "contradictions in the imperialist camp" has proved to be a rather difficult, costly, and not very productive game. Since the fall of Khrushchev, the trend in Soviet policies has been away from international revolutionary activism and toward building up Russia's own strength and influence as a global power. As Roman Kolkowicz recently observed:

> The Brezhnev regime seems to have assessed Khrushchev's policies in the Third World negatively and, abandoning the "optimistic" premises of that policy, seeks to follow a policy of "realism." This implies a more careful, orderly and pru-

---

[6] The flurry of speculation in the American press about the impending demise of Brezhnev because of his presumed commitment to detente with the United States is not relevant to our discussion. One of the basic premises of this study is that Soviet decisions are a product of consensus among Soviet leaders. It is not inconceivable that Brezhnev might be made a scapegoat for the setbacks of detente but if he is forced out, there doubtless would be other compelling considerations.

dent assessment of the costs—gains involved in the economic, military and political initiatives in the Third World. It suggests a policy that is at once tougher as well as more prudent.[7]

Soviet "prudence" in the conduct of international affairs has been repeatedly acknowledged by President Nixon, Secretaries Kissinger and Schlesinger, and other officials and public figures. This "prudence" might well be a product of the collective "realism" of the post-Khrushchev leadership, perhaps not so much in its appraisal of revolutionary potential in foreign lands as in its assessment of the capacity of the Soviet Union to harness and direct the various "anti-imperialist forces." But it also has deeper roots. Khrushchev's bombastic pronouncements—his tendency to bluff and create appearances of Soviet power and influence where little or none existed solely in order to impress "imperialists"—aside from being costly, were damaging to Soviet credibility. His "adventurism" in foreign affairs, it is to be remembered, was one of the principal charges brought against him by his comrades-in-arms.

The deliberately low profile of the present leadership may have its drawbacks in that it tempts Soviet adversaries to apply greater pressure and take tougher negotiating positions, but it also gives Soviet leaders significant advantages. They see the Soviet Union as a world power on the way up, still far away from being a showcase of prosperity, and still vulnerable to adverse pressure of the enemies. Appraising Soviet potential and world developments more conservatively, they develop a higher degree of self-confidence which translates into a flexibility which their predecessors had not possessed. They can afford tactical retreats, without worrying about "losing face." This awareness produces a caution which gives them a considerable edge over American policy makers brought up in the era of *Pax Americana* and inclined toward exaggerating United States power and influence in the world.[8]

"Realism" also means that the Soviets see their ascent in relative terms, less due to their own successes than to the decline of the might of the West. Soviet scholarly publications betray intense interest in disintegrative processes in Western societies, in weakening of political and economic ties among members of the "imperialist camp," and in

---

[7] "The Soviet Policy in the Middle East," in Michael Confino and Shimon Ahamir, *The U.S.S.R. and the Middle East* (New York: John Wiley and Sons, 1973), p. 80.

[8] One example has been wide fluctuations of U.S. attitudes toward the OPEC oil cartel, on their "hard" side bordering on fantasy. See "A New Hard Line on Oil," *Newsweek*, 7 October 1974.

Third World rebellion against the West. If a major economic depression hits the West, resulting in social turmoil and international anarchy, the Soviets may be tempted to take a more activist course in foreign affairs, especially if they perceive the need to outbid Peking in its claim to leadership of world revolutionary forces. But an effective activist policy would have to incorporate a credible readiness to embark on a collision course with the American "paper tiger," and since the Soviets do not appear disposed to take undue risks, prospects for a drastic change in their detente policy should be rated as small.

None of this analysis provides answers to the questions such as whether detente is "good" or "bad" for the United States, whether it ought to be pursued more vigorously or less, or indeed pursued at all. The external problems facing this country are staggering and we know that the Soviets (and the Chinese) can cause, aggravate or alleviate some of them. But although this may suggest that their goodwill counts, there can be no assurance that detente will produce it. Apart from the mutually recognized need to avoid dangerous confrontations and the concomitant desire to lower the level of superpower conflict, nothing in detente relationship can be taken for granted. Faced with a choice between pursuing its selfish interests or cooperating in the name of detente in partial disregard of these interests, the Soviets would unhesitatingly choose the first. To them, as to the United States, the concept of cooperation appears elusive, with no definable trade-offs, and limited to those situations where neither superpower perceives a likelihood of a loss to itself. Because they see the fundamental conflict between the two political systems as irreconcilable, national self-interest aimed at accumulation of economic strength, military power, and international influence is likely to remain at the core of both Soviet and American policies.

This is no argument against detente, but it is an argument in favor of maximum realism in appraising our own strengths and weaknesses as well as those of the adversary, and of the international environment in general. It is this appraisal, more than anything else, which would determine the course of U.S.-Soviet relations, whether "detente" remains the catchword or not.

APPENDIX

The following document, signed in Moscow on 29 May 1972, by President Nixon and General Secretary of the CC CPSU Brezhnev, represents the mutually agreed-upon framework for U.S.-Soviet detente. Many American officials have since privately expressed reservations about the restrictive interpretation of detente obligations spelled out in it as reflecting more the Soviet position and leaving out a number of issues of concern to the United States. Nevertheless, unflagging Soviet insistence on treating it as the foundation of detente leaves little room for the argument of those who want to see the agreement include other important matters.

BASIC PRINCIPLES OF RELATIONS BETWEEN THE UNITED STATES OF AMERICA AND THE UNION OF SOVIET SOCIALIST REPUBLICS

The United States of America and the Union of Soviet Socialist Republics,

Guided by their obligations under the Charter of the United Nations and by a desire to strengthen peaceful relations with each other and to place these relations on the firmest possible basis,

Aware of the need to make every effort to remove the threat of war and to create conditions which promote the reduction of tensions in the world and the strengthening of universal security and international cooperation,

Believing that the improvement of U.S.-Soviet relations and their mutually advantageous development in such areas as economics, science and culture, will meet these objectives and contribute to better mutual understanding and business-like cooperation, without in any way prejudicing the interests of third countries,

Conscious that these objectives reflect the interests of the peoples of both countries,

Have agreed as follows:

First. They will proceed from the common determination that in the nuclear age there is no alternative to conducting their mutual relations on the basis of peaceful coexistence. Differences in ideology and in the social systems of the U.S.A. and the U.S.S.R. are not obstacles to the bilateral development of normal relations based on the principles of sovereignty, equality, non-interference in internal affairs and mutual advantage.

Second. The U.S.A. and the U.S.S.R. attach major importance to preventing the development of situations capable of causing a dangerous exacerbation of their relations. Therefore, they will do their utmost to avoid military confrontations and to prevent the outbreak of nuclear war. They will always exercise restraint in their mutual relations, and will be prepared to negotiate and settle differences by peaceful means. Discussions and negotiations on outstanding issues will be conducted in a spirit of reciprocity, mutual accommodations and mutual benefit.

Both sides recognize that efforts to obtain unilateral advantage at the expense of the other, directly or indirectly, are inconsistent with these objectives. The prerequisites for maintaining and strengthening peaceful relations between the U.S.A. and the U.S.S.R. are the recognition of the security interests of the Parties based on the principle of equality and the renunciation of the use or threat of force.

Third. The U.S.A. and the U.S.S.R. have a special responsibility, as do other countries which are permanent members of the United Nations Security Council, to do everything in their power so that conflicts or situations will not arise which would serve to increase international tensions. Accordingly, they will seek to promote conditions in which all countries will live in peace and security and will not be subject to outside interference in their internal affairs.

Fourth. The U.S.A. and the U.S.S.R. intend to widen the juridical basis of their mutual relations and to exert the necessary efforts so that bilateral agreements which they have concluded and multilateral treaties and agreements to which they are jointly parties are faithfully implemented.

Fifth. The U.S.A. and the U.S.S.R. reaffirm their readiness to continue the practice of exchanging views on problems of mutual interest and, when necessary, to conduct such exchanges at the highest level, including meetings between leaders of the two countries.

The two governments welcome and will facilitate an increase in productive contacts between representatives of the legislative bodies of the two countries.

Sixth. The Parties will continue their efforts to limit armaments on a bilateral as well as on a multilateral basis. They will continue to make special efforts to limit strategic armaments. Whenever possible, they will conclude concrete agreements aimed at achieving these purposes.

The U.S.A. and the U.S.S.R. regard as the ultimate objective of their efforts the achievement of general and complete disarmament and the establishment of an effective system of international security in accordance with the purposes and principles of the United Nations.

Seventh. The U.S.A. and the U.S.S.R. regard commercial and economic ties as an important and necessary element in the strengthening of their bilateral relations and thus will actively promote the growth of such ties. They will facilitate cooperation between the relevant organizations and enterprises of the two countries and the conclusion of appropriate agreements and contracts, including long-term ones.

The two countries will contribute to the improvement of maritime and air communications between them.

Eighth. The two sides consider it timely and useful to develop mutual contacts and cooperation in the fields of science and technology. Where suitable, the U.S.A. and the U.S.S.R. will conclude appropriate agreements dealing with concrete cooperation in these fields.

Ninth. The two sides reaffirm their intention to deepen cultural ties with one another and to encourage fuller familiarization with each other's cultural values. They will promote improved conditions for cultural exchanges and tourism.

Tenth. The U.S.A. and the U.S.S.R. will seek to ensure that their ties and cooperation in all the above-mentioned fields and in any others in their mutual interest are built on a firm and long-term basis. To give a permanent character to these efforts, they will establish in all fields where this is feasible joint commissions or other joint bodies.

Eleventh. The U.S.A. and the U.S.S.R. make no claim for themselves and would not recognize the claims of anyone else to any special rights or advantages in world affairs. They recognize the sovereign equality of all states.

The development of U.S.-Soviet relations is not directed against third countries and their interests.

Twelfth. The basic principles set forth in this document do not affect any obligations with respect to other countries earlier assumed by the U.S.A. and the U.S.S.R.

Moscow, May 29, 1972

For the United States of America:

Richard Nixon
President of the United States of America

For the Union of Soviet Socialist Republics:

Leonid I. Brezhnev
General Secretary of the Central Committee, CPSU

U.S.-Soviet Detente: Past and Future by Vladimir Petrov presents antecedents of U.S.-Soviet detente and analyzes the asymmetries in national perceptions and objectives which have handicapped implementation of detente policies. Petrov discusses the bilateral aspects of detente, foreseeing extremely slow progress in SALT II negotiations and a relative regression in U.S.-Soviet economic relations. In the chapter "Detente in the World at Large," he extensively analyzes the limits of superpower cooperation in resolving the Middle East conflict and in diminishing tensions in Europe. The rest of the analysis deals with the impact of detente of the OAPEC cartel, of the "China factor," and of the Cyprus crisis.

In appraising the prospects for detente, Petrov concludes that, barring a major economic depression in the West—which would bring on severe social and political turmoil—the Soviets are likely to adhere to detente policies, continually modifying them in order to take advantage of new opportunities but firmly avoiding any direct confrontation with the United States that could result in war. The author contends that, at least for the time being, the Soviet leadership has abandoned ideologically motivated activist foreign policies, has reduced its commitment to the support of revolutionary movements, and has decided to concentrate instead on building up the economic and military might of the U.S.S.R.

Vladimir Petrov is professor of international affairs at the Institute for Sino-Soviet Studies, The George Washington University.

$3.00

American Enterprise Institute for Public Policy Research
1150 Seventeenth Street, N.W., Washington, D. C. 20036

RECENT STUDIES IN FOREIGN AFFAIRS

THE BEAR AT THE GATE: CHINESE POLICYMAKING UNDER SOVIET PRESSURE, Harold C. Hinton (112 pages, $3.00)

TROUBLED ALLIANCE: TURKISH-AMERICAN PROBLEMS IN HISTORICAL PERSPECTIVE, 1945-1971, George S. Harris (262 pages, cloth $8.50, paper $4.50)

ASIA AND THE MAJOR POWERS: IMPLICATIONS FOR THE INTERNATIONAL ORDER, Robert A. Scalapino (117 pages, $3.00)

THE CHANGING FACE OF HONG KONG: NEW DEPARTURES IN PUBLIC POLICY, Alvin Rabushka (79 pages, $3.00)

THE RATIONALE FOR NATO: EUROPEAN COLLECTIVE SECURITY—PAST AND FUTURE, Morton A. Kaplan (94 pages, $3.00)

WILL JAPAN REARM: A STUDY IN ATTITUDES, John K. Emmerson and Leonard A. Humphreys (165 pages, $3.00)

VIETNAM SETTLEMENT: WHY 1972, NOT 1969? Part I, Abram Chayes and Morton A. Kaplan; Part II, Paul C. Warnke and G. Warren Nutter; Part III, John P. Roche and Clayton Fritchey (208 pages, cloth $5.75)

AMERICAN POLICY FOR PEACE IN THE MIDDLE EAST, 1969-1971, Robert J. Pranger (69 pages, $3.00)

SOVIET ADVANCES IN THE MIDDLE EAST, George Lenczowski (176 pages, $4.00)

MAJOR MIDDLE EASTERN PROBLEMS IN INTERNATIONAL LAW, edited by Majid Khadduri (139 pages, $4.00)

DEFENSE IMPLICATIONS OF INTERNATIONAL INDETERMINACY, Robert J. Pranger (31 pages, $2.00)

THE FLOATING CANADIAN DOLLAR: EXCHANGE FLEXIBILITY AND MONETARY INDEPENDENCE, Paul Wonnacott (95 pages, $3.00)

STRATEGIC SIGNIFICANCE OF SINGAPORE, Yuan-li Wu (28 pages, $2.00)

THE EMERGENCE OF BANGLADESH: PROBLEMS AND OPPORTUNITIES FOR A REDEFINED AMERICAN POLICY IN SOUTH ASIA, Wayne Wilcox (79 pages, $3.00)

THE ARAB-ISRAELI MILITARY BALANCE TODAY, Dale R. Tahtinen (37 pages, $2.00)

ARMS IN THE PERSIAN GULF, Dale R. Tahtinen (31 pages, $2.00)

THE ARAB-ISRAELI MILITARY BALANCE SINCE OCTOBER 1973, Dale R. Tahtinen (43 pages, $2.00)

THE FUTURE OF THE CHINA MARKET: PROSPECTS FOR SINO-AMERICAN TRADE, Edward Neilan and Charles R. Smith (94 pages, $3.00)

AGREEMENT ON BERLIN: A STUDY OF THE 1970-72 QUADRIPARTITE NEGOTIATIONS, Dennis L. Bark (131 pages, $3.00)

MALAYSIA: A STUDY IN SUCCESSFUL ECONOMIC DEVELOPMENT, Wolfgang Kasper (131 pages. $3.00)

RESPONSIBLE PARENTHOOD: THE POLITICS OF MEXICO'S NEW POPULATION POLICIES, Frederick C. Turner (43 pages, $2.00)

TOWARD A REALISTIC MILITARY ASSISTANCE PROGRAM, Robert J. Pranger and Dale R. Tahtinen (48 pages, $2.00)

ARAB-AMERICAN RELATIONS IN THE PERSIAN GULF, Emile A. Nakhleh (82 pages, $3.00)

UNITED STATES DIPLOMATS AND THEIR MISSIONS: A PROFILE OF AMERICAN DIPLOMATIC EMISSARIES SINCE 1778, Elmer Plischke (201 pages, $4.00)

BRITAIN AT THE POLLS: THE PARLIAMENTARY ELECTIONS OF 1974, Edited by Howard R. Penniman (256 pages, $3.00)

Discounts: 25 to 99 copies—20%; 100 to 299 copies—30%
300 to 499 copies—40%; 500 and over—50%

THE AMERICAN ENTERPRISE INSTITUTE FOR PUBLIC POLICY RESEARCH, established in 1943, is a publicly supported, nonpartisan research and educational organization. Its purpose is to assist policy makers, scholars, businessmen, the press and the public by providing objective analysis of national and international issues. Views expressed in the institute's publications are those of the authors and do not necessarily reflect the views of the staff, advisory panels, officers or trustees of AEI.

Institute publications take three major forms:

1. **Legislative Analyses**—balanced analyses of current proposals before the Congress, prepared with the help of specialists from the academic world and the fields of law and government.
2. **Studies**—in-depth studies and monographs about government programs and major national and international problems, written by independent scholars.
3. **Rational Debates, Meetings, and Symposia**—proceedings of debates, discussions, and conferences where eminent authorities with contrasting views discuss controversial issues.

ADVISORY BOARD

Paul W. McCracken, *Chairman, Edmund Ezra Day University Professor of Business Administration, University of Michigan*
R. H. Coase, *Professor of Economics, University of Chicago*
Milton Friedman, *Paul S. Russell Distinguished Service Professor of Economics, University of Chicago*
Gottfried Haberler, *Resident Scholar, American Enterprise Institute for Public Policy Research*
C. Lowell Harriss, *Professor of Economics, Columbia University*
George Lenczowski, *Professor of Political Science, University of California, Berkeley*
Robert A. Nisbet, *Albert Schweitzer Professor of the Humanities, Columbia University*
James A. Robinson, *President, University of West Florida*

EXECUTIVE COMMITTEE

Herman J. Schmidt, *Chairman of the Board*
William J. Baroody, *President*
William G. McClintock, *Treasurer*
Richard J. Farrell
Dean Fite

SENIOR STAFF

Anne Brunsdale, *Director of Publications*
Joseph G. Butts, *Director of Legislative Analysis*
Robert B. Helms, *Director of Health Policy Studies*
Thomas F. Johnson, *Director of Research*
Gary L. Jones, *Assistant to the President for Administration*
Richard M. Lee, *Director of Planning and Development*
Edward J. Mitchell, *Director of National Energy Project*
W. S. Moore, *Director of Legal Policy Studies*
Robert J. Pranger, *Director of Foreign and Defense Policy Studies*

AEI FOREIGN AFFAIRS STUDIES

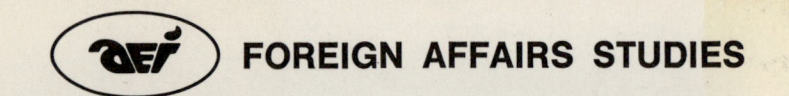

U.S.-SOVIET DETENTE: PAST AND FUTURE

Vladimir Petrov